CELEBRITY NATION

CELEBRITY NATION

HOW AMERICA EVOLVED INTO
A CULTURE OF
FANS AND FOLLOWERS

LANDON Y. JONES

BEACON PRESS
BOSTON

BEACON PRESS
Boston, Massachusetts
www.beacon.org

Beacon Press books
are published under the auspices of
the Unitarian Universalist Association of Congregations.

26 25 24 23   8 7 6 5 4 3 2 1

This book is printed on acid-free paper that meets the uncoated paper
ANSI/NISO specifications for permanence as revised in 1992.

Text design by Wilsted & Taylor Publishing Services

Library of Congress Cataloging-in-Publication Data is available
for this title.
ISBN: 978-0-8070-6565-5 (cloth)
ISBN: 978-0-8070-6566-2 (ebook)

To Sarah—
and to everyone who is curious about celebrities
(and sometimes wonders why)

CONTENTS

THE CELEBRITY-INDUSTRIAL COMPLEX

American culture is consumed by celebrity.

How did this happen? What is it doing to us? Where will it take us? How will we free ourselves from it?

None of those disquieting thoughts were in my mind when I went to work at a new magazine startup called *People* in 1974. We didn't even use the word *celebrity* then. *People*, we said, would write about both "extraordinary people" and "ordinary people who did extraordinary things."[1]

So we did. *People* had launched in March 1974, guaranteeing advertisers we would sell a million copies a week—all on newsstands. But for seventeen straight weeks, the magazine failed to achieve the million-copy promise even a single time. The cover-subject choices in those months were hit or miss—and mostly misses: Martha Mitchell, J. Paul Getty, George Wallace, Watergate judge John J. Sirica, E. Howard Hunt, Pat Nixon, Henry Kissinger, Joan Kennedy . . . This was a magazine that seemed determined to impale itself on the cross of middle age and politics. We had not yet found the magic bullet of glamorous celebrity.

Then came the eighteenth issue. On the cover was a grinning Telly Savalas, the star of the TV series *Kojak*, which had just unseated *All in the Family* as the number-one show on TV. He was bare-chested and shirtless, a look that appealed to women, many of whom wrote in demanding to see the rest of him. The combustion generated by a media exposure and a sexy star worked. *People* had its first million-seller.

Others would follow. It was 1974, the year of Watergate, and suddenly the tsunami of escapist "jiggle shows" like *Charlie's Angels*, *Wonder Woman*, and *Three's Company* were dominating television. These shows were so labelled by their critics because they featured actresses bouncing around without bras. And their fans wanted to find out more about what these actresses were like in reality.

The television stars went on the cover, one after another, as did a plethora of other famous faces. By October 1975, the magazine was averaging a million copies a week on newsstands, and by 1980, the weekly circulation was 2.5 million copies. When John Lennon died, the issue with his photo on the cover sold 2.6 million copies. By this time, *People* had suddenly become the biggest success in publishing history and conclusively legitimized a new genre: celebrity journalism, a name that once sounded like a contradiction in terms.

Celebrity was where the money was. And so, when I became the editor, I oversaw, in consecutive years, the anointment of Sean Connery, Tom Cruise, Patrick Swayze, Nick Nolte, Brad Pitt, Denzel Washington, and George Clooney as the "Sexiest Man Alive." I published a complete guide to the O. J. Simpson trial and photographs of a nearly naked Demi Moore.

But meanwhile, something was awry. I used to attend focus groups to find out what *People* readers were interested in. As the panelists settled in, the moderator would typically warm up the group by throwing out an easy question: "Who are your heroes?" But then one week at a focus group in Chicago, I noticed that the moderator no longer asked that question.

"Why don't you ask about heroes?" I asked.

"Because they can't think of any," she said.

They had no heroes? I was startled. How could that have happened? Societies need heroes and have sought them out since ancient times. Heroes are our founders and builders. A hero is a person (of any gender identity) of great deeds and great dreams who takes great risks and endures sacrifices to lead others into the future. A hero's fame cannot be manufactured; it is hard earned. Heroes give our society ballast and coherence.

We can manufacture and distribute celebrities like any other consumer products—and did so on a weekly basis at *People*. But it is not possible to create a hero. Circumstances beyond our control create heroes. Celebrities require an audience; heroes require an action. If authentic heroes attempt to reap the benefits of celebrity, there is peril—witness Charles Lindbergh, who tried to parlay his success as an aviator into a political career. Heroism is the definition of show, don't tell. The more you tell of your heroics, the less heroic you seem, and maybe are.

For most of history, celebrities and heroes have kept in their own lanes. We could tell one from the other. A celebrity can be defined as a person who is famous. We might ask of a celebrity to use their celebrity for a greater good, but we never ask an authentic hero to also sing, dance, act, and crowd into the spotlight. When they do, they tarnish a bit. Many of the celebrities I interviewed early in my career were using their fame to promote causes they saw as larger than themselves—Black nationalism (Malcolm X), pediatric AIDS (Elizabeth Taylor), and breast cancer research (Princess Diana).

This unobserved contest between celebrity and heroics is a central thread of the history I will tell here. It can be quickly stated as a variation of Gresham's law, which holds that legally undervalued currency will tend to drive legally overvalued currency out of circulation. In terms of fame, the overabundant cheap coins of celebrity have driven the limited supply of the truly heroic almost out of circulation.

Celebrities are the people we like to talk about. Our preoccupation with romanticizing celebrity has led to a coarsening of American culture and an opportunity for reality stars like the Kardashians who specialize in defiant behavior that gets them talked about. Surveys indicate that people most interested in celebrity are least engaged in politics, least likely to protest, and least likely to vote.

The boundaries between celebrities and heroes were culturally policed. Their common quality was fame, but we knew the difference. Celebrities were enjoyed, but heroes were venerated. The two were not antithetical—a celebrity could be a hero, a hero a celebrity. But we honored with awe our heroes, including the quiet ones in our midst. We still do. Think of Eugene Goodman, the Capitol Police officer who diverted the rioters from the United States Senate chamber on January 6, 2021. And Maria Ressa, the young Filipino American journalist who won the Nobel Peace Prize. Or Greta Thunberg, the Swedish teenage climate activist who was *Time*'s 2019 Person of the Year, an accolade first given to Charles Lindbergh in 1927.

If we are to encourage heroes and allow them to exert their proper and inspiring influence, we must reckon with our preoccupation with celebrity and acknowledge how it affects us both as a society and individually. The Oxford English Dictionary gives its first definition of *celebrate* as "due observance of rites and ceremonies: pomp, solemnity." Hence, Catholics "celebrate" their Mass and the priest is the "celebrant" at Communion. At heart, a celebrant provides a bridge between our workday world and something beyond it, something spiritual. People once looked to priests to do that; more recently, they have turned to celebrities to do the same, to fill them with a kind of reverence.

The problem is that what makes someone a celebrity is media exposure of their personal as well as their public lives, not their achievements. As Daniel Boorstin memorably put it in *The*

Image, written back in 1961, "*The celebrity is a person known for [their] well-knownness.*"[2] (We're looking at you, Kim Kardashian and Paris Hilton.)

Celebrity is complicated. If we define *celebrity* as a noun meaning a person who is famous, or known for their well-knownness, that's only half of the story. It is static: either you are a celebrity, or you are not. There is a bright line separating celebrities from the rest of us. In the last few decades, however, with the arrival of social media, celebrities have moved to the center of their own virtual communities, fueled by social media, and more and more fans have become micro-celebrities and, in the current argot, niche internet micro-celebrities, or acronymically, "nimcels."[3] Cultural historians Alice Marwick and danah boyd argue that celebrity has become a verb, "an organic and ever-changing *performative practice . . .* a set of circulated strategies and practices that place fame on a continuum, rather than as a bright line that separates individuals."[4]

The primary value placed on modern celebrities by their fans on social media is the appearance of accessibility and intimacy. In fact, a study at the University of San Diego found that, as the COVID-19 pandemic and social distancing dragged on into the 2020s, people maintained their "real life" friendships but felt closer to the celebrities they "liked" and "followed."[5] Could we possibly care more about the Kardashians than we care about our neighbors?

In 2000, Robert D. Putnam's *Bowling Alone: The Collapse and Revival of American Community* documented how much social structures in America—the PTA, church groups, bowling leagues—have declined since the 1960s. A dominant new medium—television—had arrived to compete for people's leisure time, followed by the internet and social media. The allure of celebrities drained the energy out of civic engagement, and celebrity worship flourished. Celebrity was a weapon of mass distraction.

I called Putnam, who agreed that "there is some kind of relationship between the decline of social capital and the rise of fame worship, especially among the young." He rightly wondered which came first—was it correlation or causation? In either case, it seems that today we are not only bowling alone but also tweeting alone, compulsively checking social media.

Constant media exposure creates a feedback loop. Because people are interested in celebrities, media cover them, and because they are constantly in the media, they attract more fans. Public visibility therefore becomes a form of mythology, part of our collective memory.

Enter, as if on cue, Donald J. Trump. Trump not only gained the nation's highest office on the strength of celebrity alone, he did so by also publicly mocking heroics. The most obvious example was his belittling of John McCain, whose courage as a naval aviator and North Vietnamese prisoner of war for five and a half years was reduced by Trump to a dismissive slur: McCain was just someone who got captured.

Like his nineteenth-century antecedents, the showmen P. T. Barnum and Buffalo Bill Cody, Trump mastered not just the messaging of celebrity but its mechanics too. He used TV and Twitter not only to grow and sustain his visibility but also to position himself as the one politician who engaged his supporters directly, unmediated by the political elite. In the absence of experience and conventional qualifications, however, he was required to work endlessly to keep reminding people he was a "totally big celebrity"—since his fame was the primary measure of his merit. Celebrity could become the loudest voice in the room.

The borderlines between public and private, ordinary and famous, famous and notorious, celebrities and heroes, have weakened or all but disappeared in recent years.

Paris Hilton, Rob Lowe, and Johnny Depp have all been involved in what would once have been career-wrecking incidents. (Hilton and Lowe were both in sex videos; Depp was accused by his ex-wife of abuse.) There was plenty of prurient interest in them, but thanks to their candor, if not remorse, there were no lasting judgments, and they have seen their greatest successes *since* then. (Depp is preparing to direct his first movie in twenty-five years.) In fact, as we will see with Hilton, a sex tape was a big part of her rise in fame and was emulated later by her friend Kim Kardashian. Their falls from grace were in fact engines for celebrity redemption.

Today's celebrity state has morphed into a vast profit-generating enterprise we can think of as the celebrity-industrial complex. It is a construct made by and for the media. Magazines like *People* were its initiators and, at first, its beneficiaries. But it spread beyond anyone's control.

There is no single model of celebrity today, thanks to the centrifugal forces of the internet and social media. Celebrities are created overnight on TikTok and Twitter. Now, an unruly democracy of celebrities crowds the public imagination. The good news is that this has opened the doors to more people who were previously marginalized, especially people of color and women. It was a short step from Archie Bunker's irascible racist character to TikTok's Filipino American star Bella Poarch and other reality show and social media stars we see now. Indeed, we can all (maybe) be celebrities. As Andy Warhol reportedly said, "In the future everyone will be famous for fifteen minutes." (More about that later.)

The question that remains is whether the job description of celebrity will retain its value and mystique in an increasingly crowded marketplace. Or will celebrity as a form of social identity start to fail? Will we return to the harder-won values of heroes—accomplishment, achievement, selflessness, inspiration—in order to find our way?

Two features of the recent history of celebrity demand our attention. The first is that while the barrier to entry to celebrity's ranks has been driven ever lower, requiring literally nothing beyond a smartphone and a YouTube account, the entry barrier to heroics remains, as it must, dauntingly high. One begs only opportunity, the other demands risk and self-sacrifice.

The second feature is celebrities' rapacious need for attention and fame. They sense, as Emily Dickinson's delightful poem explains, that . . .

> *Fame is a bee.*
> *It has a song—*
> *It has a sting—*
> *Ah, too, it has a wing.*[6]

In other words, fame can be fleeting. A heroic act can go unnoticed and remain heroic, whereas an unknown celebrity is an oxymoron. And because celebrities feed off fame, they mimic and appropriate the facsimiles of heroics. So long as we reward celebrity, we necessarily hollow out heroics.

In his books on mythology, the scholar Joseph Campbell defined what he called the great monomyth of history's dominant heroes, involving a time of separation or departure from their society, a time of terrible trial in which they discovered their vision, finding a message with which they return and share with others. I think of Moses on the mountaintop, Jesus in the desert, Odysseus at Troy, Lewis and Clark on the Western rivers, as well as the political prisoners Václav Havel and Nelson Mandela. Ultimately, they returned to the people whom they hoped to save.

While the barrier to entry for authentic heroes remains, as it must, high, access to celebrity status—the fact of public visibility and renown—has been turned upside down. We know which people are famous, but we no longer know why.

Even Hollywood, that most aristocratic of American institutions, has had to open its gates to overnight social media stars whose primary skill is not art or entertainment but, rather, the cultivation of online fame. Faced with this new breed of celebrity, the established stars in the traditional Hollywood firmament have belatedly followed suit, turning to Facebook, Twitter, TikTok, Instagram, and other platforms, including podcasts, to reclaim their audiences. The message is simple: if you are not on social media, you don't exist.

The upshot is that there is no longer a natural aristocracy of talent and charisma that establish the value of fame; it is an aristocracy of numbers—the sheer tonnage of followers, likes, retweets, Friends, and downloads. The singer Katy Perry has more followers on Twitter than there are people who live in the Philippines, Egypt, and Germany combined. This phenomenon has left the public bewildered and disoriented about the sources of celebrity and its true value. Daniel Craig once told *GQ UK*, in regard to the Kardashians, "What, you mean all I have to do is behave like a f*ing idiot on television and then you'll pay me millions?"[7]

Celebrities and the less substantive micro-celebrities bobbing in their wake will sooner or later wear out their welcome. There is some evidence this process is starting. The market for celebrity endorsements and celebrity brands has recently flattened. The oversupply of celebrities and the lack of public demand for them may have started to drive down their value, at least in areas of policy. By drawing on the history of celebrity culture and analyzing the costs we pay for it, I hope to help explain whether its current omnipresence is a temporary bubble or whether it is the beginning of a permanent sea change in the public face of fame.

If there is hope, it lies in the natural human need for heroes —and the conviction of some celebrities to take the high road. Thus, Robert Mueller refused to do interviews, press conferences, or later write a tell-all book when he led the first impeachment investigation of Donald Trump. Celebrities from Roger Federer to Michael J. Fox have enthusiastically advanced causes such as children's healthcare and Parkinson's awareness and research. The rock star Jon Bon Jovi quietly operates soup kitchens in New Jersey, for which he received an honorary degree from Princeton in 2021.

We can now see that heroes now come in all sizes and shapes, not just white males. NFL quarterback Colin Kaepernick stuck with his determination to take a knee against Black oppression, even though it cost him his career. The first gay power couple in sports—Megan Rapinoe (soccer) and Sue Bird (basketball)—have likewise kept to the high road and avoided the confessional trivialities of the media circuses.

In my later years, I have often wondered about the heroes of my youth in my hometown of St. Louis. They were my first celebrities—baseball player Stan Musial and musician Chuck Berry, both of whom I later interviewed. But the one whose memory most often stays with me is Arthur Ashe, who as a young tennis player faced racism in St. Louis and then bravely and publicly confronted his HIV-positive status as an older athlete. When I finally met him many years later, I saw a man who had surpassed celebrity. He was a hero. His example led me to write this book.

CHAPTER I

HOW IT STARTED

The certainty of meeting celebrities is that, sooner or later, you will find out how little you know about them. For me this happened the first time I met someone whom today we would call a celebrity. In the fall of 1963, I was an anxious college sophomore trying out for the staff of the student newspaper, the *Daily Princetonian*. On Wednesday, September 25, the editor said, "Jones! How would you like to interview Malcolm X?"

Malcolm X? I could not imagine anything more difficult. At the time, Malcolm was perhaps the most controversial man in America. He was the charismatic public face of the Nation of Islam (NOI), the Black Nationalist chapter of Islamic religion generally known as the Black Muslims. He had denounced all white people as evildoers. He would be coming to Princeton that afternoon from his home in New York to speak at the coffee hour of the Near Eastern Studies program.

At this time, the word *celebrity* was not in common use, especially in politics. There was no narrative of celebrity for Malcolm to "fit" into, especially as a Black man. The role that some celebrities would come to play as the agents of social change was not yet recognized. I could not imagine that the fierce Malcolm X portrayed in the media was looking forward to talking to a preppy white kid from the Ivy League.

I could not have been more wrong. The man I met had nothing to do with the man described in the media as a terrorist. He was tall, handsome, patient, with a professorial bearing, and not at all angry. He was a teacher and a very direct one. He sat with us and answered all of our questions thoughtfully and uncompromisingly.

He did not sugarcoat his beliefs—itself a violation of the then-unspoken rules of public behavior by a Black man. Instead of behaving with careful humility, as Black Americans had traditionally done, Malcolm told us that Martin Luther King's March on Washington of just a few months earlier was a "bourgeois" event conducted "by middle-class Negroes who aren't unemployed and aren't living in slums and ghettoes." He said that he saw "no distinction between [Mississippi] Governor [Ross] Barnett and [New York governor Nelson] Rockefeller as far as the treatment of the Negro is concerned. There is as much discrimination in New York as in Mississippi," except that in New York, he added, it is practiced "with a smile."[1]

Malcolm concluded by rejecting any hope of integration within America and concluded that the US government should finance the return of Black people to Africa or give them a state of their own.

What we did not know was that, at the time of our interview, Malcolm X was at a turning point in his personal life. He had become disillusioned with the NOI leader Elijah Muhammad and was disassociating himself from Muhammad's movement. He was hard at work writing *The Autobiography of Malcolm X*, driving three times a week to Alex Haley's apartment in Greenwich Village for late-night interviews for the riveting book that would be published after his death. Besides, back then, no one paid much attention to the private life of a public figure.

That would soon change. Two months after our interview, President Kennedy was assassinated. Malcolm's comment that the president's murder was the result of "the chickens coming home to roost" led to his final break with Elijah Muhammad in March 1964.[2] A month later, at a time when his views were becoming more moderate, Malcolm would make his own pilgrimage to Mecca and found his own branch of Islam. Malcolm was assassinated on February 21, 1965, while giving a speech at the Audubon Ballroom in Harlem.

Looking back on it, we saw Malcolm then through the distorted image presented in the newspapers as a near-terrorist. Today we see Malcolm's life through the fuzzy haze of popular culture. Spike Lee's 1992 film *Malcolm X* won Denzel Washington an Oscar nomination as Best Actor. Regina King's *One Night in Miami* explores Malcolm's relationship with Cassius Clay, Jim Brown, and Sam Cooke on the evening before Clay announced his conversion to Islam and took the name of Muhammad Ali.

In both of these movies, Malcolm is portrayed as a hero. This may be because his life had played out before the celebrity era had seized the public imagination. One shudders to imagine how he would have been treated in the age of social media. It is as a hero he is remembered now because that's how he is presented today in the media. But, like many people of color, Malcolm never had any control over his image as a celebrity.

The first celebrities we encounter are often the most memorable. While I was still a college student, I found myself at a symposium for what then passed for literary celebrities—Günter Grass, Susan Sontag, Eric Bentley, Leslie Fiedler, and Tom Wolfe. Suddenly I found myself looking into the bearded face of the poet Allen Ginsberg. He was dressed typically defiantly, in jeans and sweatshirt. I groped around for something to say and settled on a fatuous question of some kind to fill the silence. Ginsberg looked me over slowly, then replied, "If you ask me a sincere question, I will give you a sincere answer."

He wanted to be treated as a substantive human being, not forced into a reporter's charade of a celebrity interview. And he told me so. That was a lesson I never forgot.

Almost a decade later, on a hot June night in 1974, I stood staring down a dark corridor in the Time-Life Building in midtown New York. I was closing an article for the new magazine startup that had risen from the ashes of the recently closed *LIFE* magazine. It was called *People*, and just about everyone in the building hated it. The idea behind the magazine was to write short articles with many photos about personalities in the news—some of them well-known, but many of them not so well-known.

For my first issue I had written two articles on what we might now think of as marginal celebrities. One was on David Cassidy, a singer and teen idol from TV's *The Partridge Family* on his farewell concert tour; the other was on Marvin Zindler, a TV news reporter in Houston known mainly for his flamboyant suits.

As I stood there, one of the doors to a cubicle along the corridor flew open. A body toppled out and fell facedown, flat on the floor. As it lay there lifelessly, I realized he was Ned, a writer from *Time* who had fallen out of favor and was doing penance at *People*. He wasn't dead, just dead drunk.

The *Time* guys were particularly disdainful of *People*, which they saw as a déclassé distraction from the important issue-raising and agenda-setting they did for the nation every week. Riding in the same elevators, we heard so many disparaging comments about *People* that we took to taking the freight elevators just to avoid listening to them.

Even worse, the *Time* guys looked to be right. We thought we were tapping into a fundamental human quality: we are more interested in other people's real lives than the abstractions of policy and politics. The "People" section of *Time* was the magazine's best-read, with its publicity-generated images of celebrities attending to their rites of passage—marriages, births, and death ("Match, Hatch, and Dispatch").

Two test issues of *People*—with Elizabeth Taylor and Billie Jean King on the covers—were printed in eleven cities. Their sell-through on the newsstands—the percentage of copies purchased—was an unheard-of 80 percent. Clare Boothe Luce, the widow of Henry, reported from Honolulu that all her female friends loved it. The prospectus for the new magazine was written by Otto Fuerbringer, a former managing editor of *Time* and universally known as the Iron Chancellor. As Fuerbringer wrote: "The times seems to be right for it. The war [in Vietnam] is over. Protest is at a minimum. The counter-culture has lost much of its steam. Except for what dismay and anger Watergate stirs up, people seem to be fairly relaxed. . . . Enter *People*, reaffirming the indisputable fact that what really interests people is other people."[3]

The cover of the actual launch issue had an Old Hollywood look. It featured Mia Farrow portraying Daisy Buchanan in *The Great Gatsby*, photographed by Steve Schapiro, dressed in gauzy white, fingering her pearls and avoiding eye contact. It was remarkably similar to how Farrow's mother, actress Maureen O'Sullivan, had appeared on the cover of *Film Pictorial* in 1933.

But we quickly learned that our culture's fascination with celebrities had changed since Hollywood's golden era. Readers were more interested in Mia Farrow the woman, mother, and personality than in Mia Farrow the actress. That first issue of *People* sold an impressive 978,000 copies. That was still not enough to make the advertising rate-base guarantee, even though the article inside, written by F. Scott Fitzgerald's daughter, Scottie Fitzgerald Smith, included the salacious tidbit that Farrow became pregnant during the production (which would bring her a fourth child under the age of four) and said she heard there was "some talk of an abortion." Readers were assured that for Farrow, "that idea would have been unthinkable."[4]

The editors were groping around, trying to find the key to *monetizing* celebrity—another word we didn't often use then. The photos inside were not yet an ingratiating home take in a celebrity's house but rather studio handouts taken on the set. In one article about Hollywood, Sheilah Graham, the columnist and former companion of F. Scott Fitzgerald, mistakenly referred to herself as "a former call girl, as I was"—which led to a fiasco that was not resolved until the news editor Hal Wingo helped her correct it two weeks later to "a former chorus girl."[5] After that, we hired our first fact-checkers.

Other stories in the first issue included more authors (the Russian dissident novelist Aleksandr Solzhenitsyn, William Peter Blatty of *The Exorcist* fame) than movie stars (Mia Farrow was the only one). Solzhenitsyn was there for no reason other than Otto Fuerbringer had insisted on it. Lee Harvey Oswald's widow, Marina Oswald, was there with no news angle at all. A one-page section devoted to "The Up and Coming" featured a twenty-four-year-old rocker from Asbury Park, New Jersey, named Bruce Springsteen. "No one was smart enough to know that we didn't know what we were doing," as the founding editor Dick Stolley would wryly tell me later.

Around this time we became painfully aware of what difficult experiences had taught were the familiar six stages of a magazine launch:

FIRST STAGE:	Exultation
SECOND STAGE:	Disenchantment
THIRD STAGE:	Confusion
FOURTH STAGE:	The Search for the Guilty
FIFTH STAGE:	Punishment of the Innocent
SIXTH STAGE:	Distinction for the Uninvolved

At its heart, *People* was merchandizing an illusion. We told the public we were writing about extraordinary people. But in reality we began portraying celebrities as ordinary people. We were stripping away the mystery and mystique. Their private lives were on full display in the now-mandatory home takes requiring photographers to peek behind the curtain and reveal the subject relaxing at home, off guard with their dogs (always named), their partners, and their messy kitchens. There were no extraordinary people in this world. Everyone was recognizably ordinary.

Accordingly, we could build on this. We all are bound by the shared miseries of high school. My friend Ralph Keyes had written a charming book called *Is There Life After High School?* So *People* introduced a popular ongoing feature called "Before They Were Stars." Here were future celebrities in their geeky high school yearbook photos or flipping burgers at their summer jobs. Everyone could relate to it. The stars were just like us!

That, of course, was an illusion too.

After Watergate, Gerald and Betty Ford took up residence in the White House in August 1974. A month later, the new First Lady received a breast cancer diagnosis and underwent surgery. At that time, the press hewed carefully to a tradition of keeping their hands off the medical conditions of famous men and women alike. When Nelson Rockefeller's wife Happy had gone to the hospital for a similar radical mastectomy, the New York newspapers reported on it from a discreet distance and noted that previously mastectomies had rarely been discussed publicly or reported on at all.

Not so Betty Ford. She spoke frankly about her surgery to the news media, inviting photographers to take pictures of her in her hospital room, wearing a housecoat. "Radical mastectomy," *People* wrote in October 1974. "Suddenly, in the aftermath of Betty Ford's surgery, millions of Americans knew what it meant."

Betty Ford proceeded to rewrite the script not just for how candid First Ladies could be but also for all public figures. In a 1975 interview with *60 Minutes*, she said she wouldn't be surprised or especially concerned to hear that her daughter, then eighteen, was having premarital sex. During a televised White House tour, she noted that she and the president shared the same bed, and she told *McCall's* magazine that she slept with him there "as often as possible." Eventually, she would talk about her alcohol and painkiller addictions. For Ford, private matters were nothing to be embarrassed about. Opening up about them was honest, healthy, and, probably most importantly, potentially inspiring for millions of fellow sufferers. In her stream-of-consciousness monologues, Betty Ford set an example for candor that has never been equaled in the White House.

Soon the seesawing vagaries of magazine sales at newsstands began to provide their own feedback to the editors. Editor Dick Stolley devised his Stolley's Law of cover-subject sales:

1. Young stars sell better than old.
2. Pretty sells better than ugly.
3. Rich is better than poor.
4. TV is better than movies.
5. Movies are better than music.
6. Movies, TV, and music are all better than sports.
7. *Anything* is better than politics.

We would soon add a codicil to Stolley's Law: Nothing sells better than the celebrity dead. It was a hard lesson to learn. The tradition at Time-Life magazines was to avoid putting the recently dead on a magazine cover. When Elvis Presley died on a Monday night in 1977, *People* pushed on regardless with its scheduled cover about the actress Ann-Margret. "When I was walking down the hallway and saw staffers crying," Stolley recalled, "I realized I had made a mistake."

The first such blockbuster issue fueled by a tragedy was coverage of the death of John Lennon in 1980, followed by that of Princess Grace of Monaco in 1982. Princess Diana's death in 1997 became the magazine's all-time bestseller.

What does this tell us about the birth of modern celebrity? First, that in the 1970s, the image of celebrity was a vehicle for transporting the privileges of youth, beauty, and whiteness.

Second, that the creation of celebrities was a financial bargain made between celebrities, the media, and a willing public. For most white readers, celebrities were people who looked like them (so people of color were very rarely on the cover) and acted like them. But in truth, they were not like them.

An unspoken Stolley's Law was that white sells better than Black. Cicely Tyson was the only Black celebrity on *People*'s cover in its first year. Just one more, Muhammad Ali, was on the cover in the second year. The result was something like apartheid on the newsstands: Only two Black faces appeared as the dominant image on the *People* cover during its first ninety-five issues. In the years to come, Black people were only rarely seen on the cover: Diana Ross with her husband in 1976, Alex Haley and the then-popular O. J. Simpson in 1977, and Richard Pryor in 1978.

As time went on, readers seemed to project onto celebrities the narratives they sought in their own lives. In his book *The Redemptive Self*, Northwestern University professor Dan McAdams argues that the weekly contents of *People* demonstrate "how potent and pervasive the redemption narrative is in contemporary American society."[6]

When Dan was first telling me about his work on redemptive narratives, I said to him, "That sounds like 20 percent of the stories *People* prints."

He replied, "No, it's 52 percent. I counted."

He did, too, finding that a little more than half the stories *People* publishes share the theme of individuals moving from some "suffering to an enhanced state or situation." A dominant narrative is one many Americans define as the central objective of life: a successful struggle over adversity. They regard themselves as blessed with certain talents and advantages but then encounter obstacles and setbacks. They persevere, however, and strive to achieve their inner destiny. In the end, they justify themselves by vowing to help future generations, what Erik Erikson called "generativity."[7]

The road to the White House is paved with the narrative of redemption. Ronald Reagan had a dysfunctional family. Bill Clinton had an alcoholic father and called himself "the Comeback Kid." George W. Bush recovered from his drinking problems. Barack Obama grew up fatherless, shuttling between Hawaii, Indonesia, and Africa, and between the white and Black worlds. All of them talked freely about their sufferings and their redemptions.

Once we at *People* saw this pattern, the redemption stories flowed like a river:

Mary Tyler Moore—"Separation, Tragedy, Triumph" (1980)
Rick Nelson's family—"Tragedy & Triumph" (1991)
Shania Twain—"Triumph Over Tragedy" (1999)
J. R. Martinez—"Triumph After Tragedy" (2011)

We could now market ourselves to the stars as the good cops in a world of sleaze, a magazine that would respect their struggles and get the facts right.

Writers used to be famous. Charles Dickens was arguably the most famous writer—and entertainer—in the world when he made his American tours in the nineteenth century. He dominated the stage, reading and acting out roles and performing magic tricks. But the starlight shed by writers has more recently dimmed. As Gore Vidal told it back in 1993,

I said recently to a passing interviewer, "You know, I used to be a famous novelist." And the interviewer said, "Oh, well, you're still very well known. People read your books." And so I said, "I'm not talking about *me*. I'm talking about the category. 'Famous novelist'? The adjective is inappropriate to the noun. It's like being—'I'm a famous ceramicist.' Well, you can be a good ceramicist. You can be a rich ceramicist. You can be much admired by other ceramicists. But you aren't famous. That's gone."[8]

In the 1980s, the celebrities and their entourages of publicists began an organized pushback against the media—and the war over control and access began. The result at *People* was the creation of new journalistic tools. The following terms were invented to describe them:

One was the *write-around.* If we had no access, no quotes, no photos, then it was no problem. We did a write-around—an attempt to create a narrative mainly from newspapers and using quotes from interviews with people only tangentially involved with the actual story. They were called *tertiaries* or just *terts.*

Another was *the swarm.* The best way to gather the factoids needed for a write-around was to assign as many reporters as possible to report and interview as many sources as possible. We swarmed the story just as voraciously as a swarm of wasps would go after their prey.

The swarms and write-arounds could be about anyone, but most were about the British royals or anyone in the Kennedy family. Movie stars not willing to give interviews could include the likes of Leonardo DiCaprio. As one reporter told me later, "I was once asked to hang out in Leonardo's hotel lobby during the London Film Festival in the hope that I would grab him as he wobbled in from whatever parties he'd been to. I pointed out to my bureau chief that hotel managements tended to frown on lone women hanging out in the lobby for hours on end with no apparent purpose beyond eyeing up any men who came through the door. I could have told them that I was working, but working girls are exactly who they wanted to discourage."

Weddings were almost always write-arounds. So if Michael Jackson marries Lisa Marie Presley, no problem—someone will talk. Likewise Brooke Shields and Andre Agassi, JFK Jr. and Daryl Hannah. As for tracking the late queen, Elizabeth II, reporters covered her family like poachers track exotic species in the veldt. London correspondent Laura Sanderson Healy once saw the queen at the Royal Ascot races and said, "You could roam around her and other people out by the horses. I did a lot of my reporting of the royals that way, just observing them like Jane Goodall did her chimpanzees in the jungle, studying them. That's what it felt like."[9] It was a dance that humans have known for centuries. Even if the celebrities want to stay out of the spectacle, the spectacle will find them.

CHAPTER 2

BREAD AND CIRCUSES

The History of Fame

Celebrity is a problem with a past.

We can look at fame as a constant throughout history, something in the air, invisible and always there, like gravity. We all respond to it, no matter whether it is in the guise of fame or heroes, frauds or celebrities.

We can think of celebrity as an agent of mythology since classical times. The ancients manufactured their celebrities in the forms of the gods and goddesses. The psychic mechanism that led the Greeks to project their needs onto the gods was their attempt to understand the unknowns around them—alchemy, astrology, mythology—what Carl Jung called the archetypes of the collective unconscious. The British classical scholar Jane Ellen Harrison said that the early gods represented projections of a group's identity—its fears, wishes, dreams.

It is accompanied by both celebration and condemnation. In his tenth satire, in the year 120 CE, the Roman poet Juvenal used the phrase *panem et circenses*, or "bread and circuses," to describe the public's embrace of the trivial. Juvenal wrote that "the public has long since cast off its cares; the people that once bestowed commands, consulships, legions and all else, now meddle no more and long eagerly for just two things—Bread and Circuses!"[1]

Then, as now, the public has often found its circuses in its embrace of celebrities. There have always been well-known people. They used to owe their fame to their talents and their accomplishments. But there has also always been the taint of the bogus.

Since the Enlightenment, advances in science and thought have stripped away the places where the ancients could see the gods and goddesses at work, so we are left with the imagined lives of celebrities to draw on. The Greeks knew that we needed to see their gods as flawed; they stumbled and revealed our humanity to us. Tragic heroes are flawed, making them tragic.

When a great man or woman appeared, people looked for God's purpose in them. One of the primary characteristics we see in both the ancient gods and today's celebrities is our common perception of what Rudolf Otto calls "numinosity" in his book *The Idea of the Holy*. He defines it, in part, as "creature feeling. . . . It is the emotion of a creature, abased and overwhelmed by its own nothingness in contrast to that which is supreme above all creatures."[2] Venus was revered, and statues of Aphrodite were everywhere. Great men and women and famous men and women were pretty much the same people.

But some of today's patterns are there, including the shared suspicions of earthly fame. In Odysseus's most celebrated adventure on his voyage home to Ithaca, he tells the giant Cyclops that his name is Nobody. Then, when Odysseus gouges out Cyclops's eye, the giant bellows, "Nobody is killing me!"

Both celebrities and gods disguise themselves. When he is finally home, Odysseus dresses as a tramp to deceive Penelope's suitors—a pattern of behavior celebrities continue to emulate in efforts to shed the artifice of fame. Greta Garbo pleads behind her dark glasses: "I want to be left alone." As we shall see, the famous can learn only when they divest themselves of celebrity.

Throughout most of human history, fame has been seen as a positive—something achieved by exceptional behavior. Here lie our heroes: Alexander the Great, Julius Caesar, Cleopatra, Jesus, Muhammad, Joan of Arc, Shakespeare. In his exhaustive study, *The Frenzy of Renown,* cultural critic Leo Braudy identifies Alexander the Great as "the first famous person."[3] But Alexander achieved lasting fame only posthumously as the first mortal face to be placed on a coin (perhaps the first instance of a new technology being used to promote celebrity).

If there was a difference between fame and celebrity, it was not clear then. Heroes were *celebrated.* The word was most often used as a verb. Celebrity was a temporary condition; fame was lasting. In the time of the Renaissance, fame was assigned only to a few royals, religious figures, and renowned artists like Michelangelo and Leonardo.

Celebrity was the condition of being famous; but being celebrated was not the same thing as being a celebrity. A *celebrity* as a certain category of person, separate and apart from his or her achievements, had yet to be invented.

Not until the eighteenth century and the beginning of the Romantic age did the word *célébrité* emerge as a noun—referring to poets, chefs, actors—almost all men. Since most historians then were men, it is not surprising that the celebrities they saw were also men. As the French aphorist Nicolas Chamfort put it, celebrity was "the privilege of being known by people who don't know you."[4] In Paris, the author Jean-Jacques Rousseau was horrified to find himself surrounded by crowds when he played chess in a cafe or took a walk in the Tuileries. Well before Greta Garbo, Rousseau was one of the first to denounce the loss of privacy and control of his private life resulting from his fame.

One of the first uses of the word *celebrity* in a robustly secular sense was by Dr. Samuel Johnson, one of the most renowned men of his time. He wrote in 1751: "I did not find myself yet enriched in proportion to my celebrity."[5] But, as he would later acknowledge, "When once a man has made celebrity necessary to his happiness, he has put it in the power of the weakest and most timorous malignity, if not to take away his satisfaction, at least to withhold it."[6]

In his sweeping study of the rise of charismatic leadership during the era of great revolutions between 1725 and 1820, historian David A. Bell argues that the Enlightenment and military adventurism transformed the relationship between people and their leaders. Drawing on the lives of George Washington, Napoleon, Toussaint Louverture, and Simón Bolívar, Bell observes that the media revolutions of the period—engraving technologies that could reproduce recognizable faces and books reporting on the private lives of leaders—amounted to creating celebrities, just as that word was coming into use. Citizens felt they had a new bond with leaders, as if they knew them as "friends."[7]

Once the mechanisms of celebrity were in place, these self-styled men on horseback became godlike in their stature. (Women like Catherine the Great did not qualify since they were not military leaders.) Their reputations leaped beyond the frames of the heroic paintings by Jacques-Louis David and Charles Willson Peale.

George Washington was the object of countless ephemera, many of them spurious. Within weeks of Washington's death, a thirty-year-old bookseller and preacher named Mason Locke Weems published his fanciful *Life of George Washington*, filled with heroic tales about the president (the cherry tree, for example). Bell describes it as establishing "the measure of charisma against which all subsequent American political figures have to live up to."[8] Thanks to Weems, and Boswell in England, the emerging new technology of illustrated books was linked with charismatic leadership. Napoleon, Louverture, and Bolívar now had their role model.

In life, of course, Washington was not so willing to embrace his worldwide fame, which made his reputation all the more formidable. A highborn woman who had met him later wrote, "You must know that I have had the happiness . . . of seeing this incomparable President. You may laugh but he has a most beautiful face. Did you ever see a countenance a thousandth part so expressive of that goodness, benevolence, sensibility, and modesty which characterize him?" He was not an angel, she said, "But he is a man, and we feel proud of it."[9] In other words, the human characteristics that define a celebrity were present, along with godliness.

One popular story held that the prominent statesman Gouverneur Morris accepted a dare from Alexander Hamilton to approach the aloof Washington at a reception and greet him with a slap on the back. Morris did and was rewarded by a withering stare from Washington. The abashed Morris later said he would not do it again for a thousand dinners. But stories like that enabled Americans to find a personal bond with Washington in a way that even portraits could not.[10]

By the middle of the eighteenth century, this novel way of perceiving prominent personalities had spread beyond military leaders to actors, clergy, musicians, writers, and politicians. Celebrity had a weaker meaning than renown or fame, but it was already a force to be reckoned with. For example, in October 1740, a twenty-five-year-old Anglo-American boy-wonder preacher named George Whitefield climbed onto a platform on the Boston Common to address a crowd of twenty thousand. It was thought to be the largest gathering in the history of the American colonies. According to his most recent biographer, Thomas S. Kidd, the young evangelist was then the most famous man in America—and the most famous man in Britain, too, aside from the king. In short, before his fame waned, "he was the first modern transatlantic celebrity of any kind," writes Kidd. "With apologies to the Beatles, George Whitefield was the first 'British sensation.'"[11]

The cultural forces that were coming together during the Enlightenment—commercial printing presses and the creation of mass audiences—grew more intense during the Romantic period at the end of the eighteenth century and the first half of the nineteenth century. George Gordon Byron, who would go into history as Lord Byron, famously said upon the publication of *Childe Harold's Pilgrimage* in 1812: "I awoke one morning and found myself famous."[12] He became one of the first celebrities to ride on the winds of his own notoriety, cultivating scandal the way Madonna or Cardi B or Billie Eilish do now.

The original identity structure for celebrity was all male and all white. The performer Franz Liszt became the most famous face in Europe as a result of his tours, beginning in 1844. Writers like Charles Dickens and later Mark Twain could promote themselves with their tours of America. They were considered celebrities because of their achievements—their books, adventures, talents, even deeds—not only because of their public visibility. Another touring writer, Oscar Wilde, cultivated his celebrity by his flamboyant clothing styles and provocative sexuality. He paved the way for later defiant celebrities like Boy George and David Bowie.

Celebrity arrived in America emphatically in the nineteenth century with the appearance of the impresarios like Phineas Taylor Barnum—P. T. Barnum—who was one of the first to reap profits from it. The selling of celebrity became the engine that developed it—usually at the expense of others.

Barnum began his career by exhibiting people of color in satirical and degrading ways—capitalizing on their fame and blurring it with notoriety. The first was an elderly Black woman named Joice Heth. Barnum leased her as a slave for $1,000 and proclaimed that she was 161 years old and the former nurse of George Washington. He similarly exploited "living curiosities" such as the diminutive General Tom Thumb—born Charles Stratton—who was just five years old, stood an inch over two feet tall, and danced and sang "Yankee Doodle" in Barnum's show. There was also a helpless Black man with an unusual head shape whom Barnum proclaimed to be "a creature, found in the wilds of Africa . . . a kind of man-monkey."[13] To Barnum, the self-styled "Prince of Humbugs," walking the line between fact and fiction was business as usual. Celebrity was a fake, a mass illusion he invented for the public's amusement and his own riches.

Barnum's most successful celebrity was not a humbug, however. She was the singer Jenny Lind, "the Swedish nightingale." When he imported the twenty-nine-year-old Lind from Europe in 1850, she was greeted at the shipyard docks by thirty to forty thousand cheering New Yorkers. The "Lindomania" gave Barnum an aura of borrowed operatic prestige, as the electrifyingly talented Lind toured the country, drawing enormous crowds. She was a celebrity who was made into a product, giving up to two hundred performances a year before the rising urban middle class in an industrializing America. She was greeted with the same adoration that Frank Sinatra and Elvis Presley enjoyed in the 1950s and Rihanna, Nicki Minaj, and Taylor Swift would receive years later.

Celebrity as a form of public entertainment and public mythology grew further in the second half of the nineteenth century with the arrival of Sarah Bernhardt. Born in Paris in 1844, she became famous throughout France as an actress in the Théâtre Français. As Sharon Marcus points out in her study of the star, Bernhardt cultivated her image as an unconventional, outspoken rebel and used the new technology of reproducible halftone photography to her advantage.[14] She was photographed melodramatically throughout her career, in both her stage roles and even sleeping in a coffin in her bedroom. She toured America to widespread attention everywhere she went.[15]

Ever since the first daguerreotypes in the nineteenth century, observers had noticed photography's potential to bring loved ones, dear or distant, into every household (as well as, inevitably, pornography). Moreover, the act of viewing the physiognomy of leaders like Abraham Lincoln offered both inspiration and moral edification. The photographic image was associated with fame from the beginning.

During the Civil War, small albumen prints mounted on a 2¼-inch by 4-inch paper card and called cartes de visite ("visiting cards") became a national craze. They had been patented and popularized in 1854 by a Frenchman, André-Adolphe-Eugène Disdéri, and imported to America. Photographers like Mathew Brady saw in the cartes de visite an opportunity to inspire citizens with the noble visages of their political and religious leaders, "the great and the good, the heroes, saints, and sages."[16] Families collected them in albums by the thousands and exchanged them with friends and collectors. In 1860, Brady created a carte de visite of the eighteen-year-old Prince Albert Edward, Prince of Wales, who was greeted by a crowd of a half million on the first visit of an English royal to the United States.

But while Brady was focused on photographing families and political elites, he missed the opportunity the cartes de visite presented to reach a mass audience. That would fall to a French Canadian, Napoleon Sarony, who specialized in popular theatrical stars and used the slightly larger cabinet-card size of 4 by 6½ inches. The new cards allowed more detail in the portraits of faces and demonstrated that actors could imitate the physiognomy of the nobility. Among others, Sarony photographed Oscar Wilde, Lillie Langtry, Edwin Booth, and Sarah Bernhardt. His portraits of the American actress Adah Isaacs Menken were considered sensational due to her erotic costuming and voluptuous poses on the floor. Soon, Sarony began paying large fees to his celebrities for the privilege of their posing for him. He eventually boasted of having a collection of forty thousand theatrical portraits for sale. At the same time, his photographs of the actress Lillie Langtry were commanding good prices, his portraits of politicians like Grover Cleveland were not selling at all.[17]

What it amounted to was that the vanished photographers who pioneered the new technology of the cartes de visite had established something new in our culture: the primacy of the celebrity image. As historian Barbara McCandless observes,

"The portrait photographers who created this huge popular market thus became expendable, a quaint reminder of an earlier time when the American public was dependent upon a small group of professional photographers for the manufacture of public faces that could inspire and entertain."[18]

Among the first to capitalize on the new cartes de visite was the showman William Frederick Cody—better known as Buffalo Bill. Cody based his career on fanciful tales of his frontier exploits as a Pony Express rider and Indian scout that were largely fabricated. His contributions to the lore of the cowboy West were broadcast widely through his Buffalo Bill's Wild West traveling show. In its reenactments, hatchet-wielding Native Americans were displayed as the enemies of god-fearing American settlers. The flamboyant show toured the United States and, in 1889, Great Britain, France, Barcelona, Sardinia, Naples, Rome, and Florence. In 1891, the show went on to Germany, Holland, Belgium, Scotland, Wales, and back to London.

Celebrity was linked with mythology from Achilles to Buffalo Bill. Thanks to the images presented in cartes de visite and later in programs and posters, Cody was said to be the most recognizable celebrity in the world, outside royalty. His world of show business blurred with politics—a sign of things to come. In 1892, the periodical *People's Press* proclaimed,

> Buffalo Bill is one of the most remarkable men of his time. He has not been spoiled by military success at home, or by being lionized abroad. He is still a young man, and a thoroughly representative American. Outside a number of plutocrats who never like to see a man of the people rise, "Buffalo Bill" is one of the best known and most highly esteemed of America's citizens. His home is in Nebraska, the state wherein the People's Party will gather to nominate a candidate for President of the United States. They cannot take a man from either of the two old parties, and they will be hard pushed for a man at once possessing the essentials, nerve, intelligence, integrity

and popularity. What better could be done than to nominate the gentleman from Nebraska, who is honored by the nations, Hon. W. F. Cody?[19]

Although African Americans and Mexican Americans played central roles in Western expansion, Cody did not use his celebrity-making machinery to display their participation. Instead, their presence in the West was completely erased in his shows. Native Americans were portrayed as savages, and women appeared only rarely in the guise of mock-heroines like Annie Oakley.

Cody specifically used the tradition of blackface minstrel shows that had existed in America since the 1820s. His co-sponsored show, Black America, hired hundreds of Black performers who demonstrated how to work a cotton gin, sang the racist ditty "Old Black Joe," and did demeaning cakewalks.

Cody used his own autobiography, published in 1879, to conjure up a myth of a frontier West that was already disappearing. As Joy Kasson vividly documents in her *Buffalo Bill's Wild West: Celebrity, Memory, and Popular History*, Cody based his traveling show on illusion, not reality. A staple of his show was a reenactment of the Battle of the Little Big Horn that ended with Cody himself riding triumphantly into the arena strewn with bodies, commemorating an American victory that never happened.

We can now see that Cody created his celebrity to help Americans find heroes to justify their presence on the frontier. In England, Queen Victoria saw the Wild West show, and the Duke of Windsor shook hands with Annie Oakley. Kasson reports that Cody's only rival as the most famous American, Mark Twain, saw the show in 1885 and wrote to Cody that he "enjoyed it thoroughly. . . . The show is genuine . . . the same as I saw on the frontier years ago."[20]

Like Lord Byron before them, Samuel Clemens and William Cody both used adopted stage names for their alter egos and

added distinctive styles of dress to brand themselves as celebrities—Twain with his white suits and cigar, Buffalo Bill with
buckskins and a Winchester rifle. That sartorial touch has lived
on among celebrities. When Theodore Roosevelt traveled to
North Dakota, he borrowed the dress style of buckskins from
Cody and later took his Rough Riders moniker from the Wild
West show.

As Kasson summarizes it:

> Buffalo Bill's success was at its height in 1893. He was a ce-
> lebrity in the modern sense of the word: a well-known per-
> son who attracted public attention as much for who he was
> as for any particular deeds or accomplishments. But even as
> he reached the peak of his career, his highly crafted persona
> began to take on a reality of its own, and the human being
> was increasingly hard put to keep his life in harmony with his
> public image. While Buffalo Bill reassured his audiences that
> the old values of individual heroism could tame the wilder-
> ness of emerging modernity, William Cody struggled with
> problems of excess and chaos in his personal finances, his
> marriage and love life, and his corporate identity.[21]

Like Twain, Barnum, and then Donald Trump more than
a century later, Cody wanted to be an entertainment star and
a successful businessman. And like Barnum and Trump, Cody
never had the resources to match his style of living. He was
eventually discredited by divorce, sexual shenanigans, drunkenness, and bankruptcy before he died in 1917.

A contemporary of Cody's often identified with him as a
breakthrough celebrity was Martha Jane Canary, who called
herself Calamity Jane. Born in Missouri, she created her own
stand-alone frontier myth, adopting a tough, cross-dressing
public identity that cultural critic Jack Halberstam later called
"female masculinity."[22] She never worked for Cody, but, as the
historian Karen Jones documents, she drew on the same myths

of frontier scouting, gun and horse skills, and pulp fictions to create an entertainment career.[23] Calamity was a belligerent, cigar-smoking performer who fit the moniker she adopted and was the model of today's defiant female celebrities, like disability rights activists Judy Heumann and Alice Wong, and Black Lives Matter founders Patrisse Cullors, Alicia Garza, and Ayo (formerly Opal) Tometi.

As we shall see, for later celebrities ranging from Cary Grant (Archibald Leach) to Bob Dylan (Robert Zimmerman) to Lady Gaga (Stefani Joanne Angelina Germanotta), stage names are personal brands that distinguish them amid the cacophony of rivals. The cultural critic Fintan O'Toole describes George Bernard Shaw's omnipresent initials of GBS as the "invention of a single, obscure impoverished Irishman . . . one of the great achievements of the history of advertising," which produced a "unique form of celebrity: a vast popularity that depended on a reputation for insisting on unpopular ideas and causes, for pleasing the public by provoking it to the point of distraction."[24]

The name and reputation of Calamity Jane were largely her invention. According to Karen Jones, Martha Canary's autobiography, *The Life and Adventures of Calamity Jane, by Herself* (1896), is "hokum, an exercise in creative writing and myth-making."[25] She never scouted for General Custer nor was she ever a Pony Express rider. What she did do was challenge the assumptions of gender normality that were central to the myth of frontier masculinity.

In Barnum's time, theater was the one scaffold a woman could use to climb to fame. Jenny Lind and Sarah Bernhardt did it, as did Annie Oakley. Calamity Jane appeared in the Pan-American Exposition in Buffalo, New York, in 1901. She charged into it by driving a team of one hundred mules down the main street, following up with riding and gunplay tricks. She was later jailed for drunkenness and forced to make her way back to Montana by appearing in tawdry dime museum shows en route.

Martha Jane Canary died on August 1, 1903. The popular legend that she'd had a romance with Wild Bill Hickok seemed generated mainly to make her nonconformist gender behavior less threatening. She knew Hickok for only three months. But that was enough for Hollywood to use the myth in the movie versions of her life, the best known of which is David Butler's 1953 musical starring, of all people, the perky and brightly feminine movie star Doris Day.

Calamity Jane's celebrity eventually propelled her into TV Westerns, notably in a 1966 episode of *Death Valley Days* titled "A Calamity Called Jane." The plotline continues the mixture of celebration and critique so familiar in the twentieth century. Here, Jane joins Buffalo Bill's Wild West show only to be told to act more like a lady.

The frontier mythology of rough-hewn masculinity that lifted so many actors to celebrity did so most successfully for the affable host of *Death Valley Days* in 1964–65, future president Ronald Reagan. Reagan occupies an ambiguous place in the celebrity universe. He was initially a conventional movie star celebrity, known for his middlebrow Westerns and comedies like *Bedtime for Bonzo*. Hosting *Death Valley Days* on television, he rode in on the masculine myth of the vanishing frontier West that had propelled Buffalo Bill to become the Most Famous American of his time, according to his biographer Joy Kasson. But then, as California's governor and a US president, Reagan was something else altogether. He was more substantive than a show-biz celebrity, but something less than a hero.

On January 17, 1984, I was invited to attend a luncheon discussion in the Cabinet Room of the White House with President Reagan and a variety of private-sector leaders on the topic of government policies affecting American families. I was invited, thanks to my 1980 book *Great Expectations*, on the generation I had whimsically named baby boomers. The other participants included then vice president George H. W. Bush; Bush's chief of staff, James Baker; and a gallimaufry of writers, scholars, and religious leaders, mostly male and all white. They must have wondered why the editor of *People* was there in the same meeting with James Dobson, the evangelical radio broadcaster.

Sitting around the cabinet table, each of us presented our ideas for five minutes or so. I posited that the government should devise policies to accommodate American families who, in reality, were "more diverse than the breadwinner/housekeeper model set in stone by *Ozzie and Harriet*." I hoped to get the president's attention by mentioning the familiar Nelson family he knew well. But in response he said not a word about the comments made by any of the participants. Instead, he launched into his hackneyed campaign rhetoric about the "welfare queens" driving Cadillacs while living on food stamps.

The luncheon was followed by a receiving line and photo ops. To my surprise, at one point I noticed that the president was standing alone, apart from the crowd, awkwardly smiling and shifting his weight from foot to foot. No one was willing to break the ice to approach him. I saw not a president but the aw-shucks narrator of *Death Valley Days*. I felt sympathy for him, of all things. So I eased over toward him, preparing to make small talk. Suddenly a Secret Service man stepped out of nowhere and blocked me. "Move on!" he said tersely. I did.

What did this teach me?

First, that we know nothing about the real nature of celebrities. Malcolm X had surprised me with his gentleness and responsiveness. Later, Princess Diana would impress me with her approachability. Ronald Reagan was the opposite. He still relied on the highly controlled public settings that gave him control and protected him. He lived by the same illusions that Bill Cody and Calamity Jane had created in their time—and Bill Cosby did in ours. He wasn't a president; he just played one on TV.

Second, embarrassingly, I seemed to want him to acknowledge me—a need for connection the public has burdened celebrities with since the time of Jean-Jacques Rousseau and Voltaire. The more famous the person, the more intimate the relationship fans and the press think they are entitled to. Just as stalkers and crazed fans pursued Sarah Bernhardt, and the press reported on her every move, so did we with Ronald Reagan. In reality, he was socially awkward and intellectually vacant.

I was finally beginning to understand celebrities.

CHAPTER 3

THE DARK SIDE OF CELEBRITY

The modern character of celebrity flowered early in the twentieth century after the introduction of photographs in newspapers and magazines. The media's ability to reprint stories with images and constant repetition of the visual details, not the deeds, was the key to redirecting the public's attention. Now the public could explore their celebrities' habitats, no matter if it was the Cathay Hotel in Shanghai or the Café Carlyle, Studio 54, and, currently, Zero Bond in downtown Manhattan. These places could be described, as Shanghai was at the time, as "heaven on top of hell."[1]

The dark side of fame can be horribly dark. As Emily Dickinson said, it has a sting. The famous attract the psychopathic, who not only believe they know you but also know all about you, even where you live. Two horrible events stand out: the grisly murder of actress Sharon Tate in 1969 and the shooting of John Lennon in 1980.

Politicians are also among the vulnerable. They want to have a following. They espouse a message, but not everyone approves of the message. The threat of assassination is always present. Bodyguards are not always effective. The Kennedys, Martin Luther King Jr., Abraham Lincoln, leaders around the world from

Julius Caesar to Mahatma Gandhi met their fates because there are always people who hate what others say or perhaps want to become famous as a politician's killer.

Mass shootings sometimes take place because the seriously despondent person who wants to commit suicide decides to have a moment of fame by posting their savage rampage on social media.

Philosophy and science also have had their superstars, and some attain superstar status posthumously: Socrates was forced to have a bit of hemlock as his former fans looked on. Galileo's incredible contributions only got him into trouble during his lifetime: opposition from the Catholic Church, which eventually tried Galileo through the Inquisition and forced him to spend the rest of his life under house arrest.

Fame can be a hard pill to swallow. Robert Oppenheimer was placed on a precarious public pedestal for his participation in the development of the atom bomb. As he witnessed the first nuclear explosion, he later said he remembered a line from the Hindu *Bhagavad Gita*, "Now I am become Death, the destroyer of worlds."[2] When I saw Oppenheimer accepting an honorary degree in the last year of his life, he still looked haunted.

The public follows their celebrities even through their dark times. The trials of O. J. Simpson and, recently, Johnny Depp and Amber Heard captivated audiences for weeks as the courthouse became their default stage.

The death of the silent-screen star Rudolph Valentino in 1926 at the age of thirty-one created what was then the first media frenzy around a modern celebrity with tens of thousands of mourners in the streets. But that attention-grabbing event was overshadowed a year later by Charles Lindbergh's historic flight across the Atlantic on May 21, 1927. It was an act of authentic heroism—he went where no one had successfully gone before, he went alone, and he had a vision.

Thanks to the media, all of the modern world could now participate in a public event for the first time ever.[3] Lindbergh was followed obsessively by radio, telephones, radiography, newsreels, and undersea cables. As Scott Berg documents in his Pulitzer Prize–winning biography, at the age of twenty-five the boyish Lindbergh had become "the most celebrated living person ever to walk the earth."[4] In New York, the parade for him was led by ten thousand soldiers and sailors. Some three hundred thousand people greeted him in the Sheep Meadow of Central Park. In Brooklyn, seven hundred thousand turned out, straining to see the handsome face they had already seen in the newspapers. In Washington, Lindbergh gave a radio address to an estimated eight hundred thousand people. He later traveled all over Europe and the US. When he flew to Latin America, one newspaper editor wired to his reporter, "No more stories unless he crashes!" Even before his flight Lindbergh had cut endorsement deals with Mobile Oil, AC Spark Plugs, and Wright Aeronautical.

Lindbergh hated it. The price was that he lost his privacy and freedom of movement. He wanted to keep his private life private and broke what was already the unwritten rule of celebrity: You had to accept it.

Five years later, all that would change. On Tuesday, March 1, 1932, Lindbergh's twenty-month-old son, Charles Lindbergh Jr., was taken from his crib in the second-floor nursery of the family's newly completed home, Highfields, in Hopewell, New Jersey. Seventy-two days later, on May 12, after a failed ransom exchange, the toddler's body was found just four miles from the Lindbergh home.

Reporters and tourists descended on the hapless Lindberghs. Photos surreptitiously taken of the baby's corpse in the Trenton morgue sold for $5 apiece. Charles and Anne retreated to her family's estate in Englewood, New Jersey, to no avail. When their little dog ran away, Lindbergh pursued him—only to find himself pursued by eight reporters. Anne plaintively wondered if not for the press attention that had always surrounded them whether "we might still have [our baby]."[5]

It wasn't until September 1934—over two years later—that Bruno Richard Hauptmann was arrested in the Bronx after paying for his gasoline with ransom money.

No media event before then had approached the scale of the relentless, circus-like coverage of the ensuing trial. By the time Hauptmann's trial started, in January 1935, all eyes were on the county courthouse in the rural town of Flemington, New Jersey. The main street outside its doors was overwhelmed by press and sightseers alike. In a single day, Berg estimates, more than six thousand tourists and gawkers were roaming the streets.

For the first time, photographic images found their way into widely distributed newspapers. The leading reporters and commentators of the day were also there: Damon Runyon, Walter Winchell, Dorothy Kilgallen, Sheilah Graham, Alexander Woollcott. The *New York Times* published transcripts of each day's testimony. There were ominous signs that the division between news and entertainment was weakening, as witness the presence of the comedian Jack Benny. A store in Flemington sold 1,300 replicas of the ladder allegedly used in the kidnapping.

On the trial's second day, Charles Lindbergh testified. He described the night of April 2, 1932, when he accompanied intermediary Dr. Condon to the edge of St. Raymond's Cemetery in the Bronx, New York, with the ransom money and heard a voice call out, "Hey, Doctor!" Turning and looking directly at the defendant from the witness stand, Lindbergh unequivocally identified that voice as Hauptmann's. The crowd gasped, and for many, the case was closed—even though the trial would go on for another thirty days, with a total of 157 witnesses questioned.

On February 13, 1935, at 11:15 a.m., the prosecution and defense rested their cases. The thirty-two-day trial was over, and the jury retired to decide the fate of Richard Hauptmann. Thousands gathered outside the courthouse as they deliberated. As the sun set, the press installed floodlights so the news cameras could get their shot at any time. Then, at 10:38 p.m., the courthouse bell tolled, signaling a decision.

The verdict: murder in the first degree. The sentence: death, with execution already set for the week of March 18. From the start, jurors had been unanimous in finding Hauptmann guilty; the only need for deliberation was for penalty. When the crowd heard that Hauptmann would die, they roared in approval. After a number of failed appeals, Hauptmann was executed in the electric chair on April 3, 1936. Hauptmann maintained his innocence until the end.

Much of Charles Lindbergh's life afterwards amounted to a long effort to avoid and deny his celebrityhood. But as World War II loomed, Lindbergh's celebrity status led him to seize the opportunity to become a spokesman for the unpopular position of those who wanted to stay out of the war. By seeking to trade on his celebrity status—articulating not the sense of mission that guided him across the Atlantic, but a divisive and unpopular political position that was opposed by a majority of Americans—his credibility as a hero was forever tarnished. (Today, of course, not even Lindbergh would be able to protect the secret of his three mistresses and seven children in Germany from the scrutiny of the tabloids and social media.)

In early October 1953, my hometown in St. Louis was a cradle of musical history—New Orleans jazz, ragtime, Chicago blues, country and western had all migrated there on the Mississippi. Three actual turn-of-the-century crimes in St. Louis gave birth to three of America's best-known crime ballads—"Frankie and Johnny," "Duncan and Brady," and "Stackolee"—all about murders. The homegrown Josephine Baker and Miles Davis had each decamped for the East and then Europe, but, in 1951, Ike Turner recorded "Rocket 88"—the first true rock and roll song—with Jackie Brenston, and Ike's Kings of Rhythm were the most popular soul band in the city, even before Tina arrived. On New Year's Eve 1952, a Sumner High School kid named Chuck Berry played for the first time with his pianist Johnnie Johnson at the Cosmopolitan Club in East St. Louis—and rock's most characteristic crossover sound was born.

I was attending Clark School, the same elementary school where Ntozake Shange—writing in the voice of her novel's titular character Betsey Brown—remembered the floors "shining like the halls of Tara."[6] Exactly a month before my tenth birthday, I began selling tickets to the Boy Scout circus door to door in the urban streets near our apartment. It was a busy area—the streetcars rattling up and down Waterman Avenue would trace moving lattices of light across the ceiling of my bedroom every night.

In those days, my mother and father had no qualms about sending a little boy out to work the neighborhood with a change purse and a fistful of circus tickets. I could cover a lot of ground in a short time. I would knock on doors up and down Waterman, with its stolidly middle-class brick apartment houses, repeating my spiel: "Hello, I am selling tickets to the Boy Scout circus. How many tickets would you like?"

The big payoff was from the rich people who lived in the gated streets with rococo mansions that dated to the 1904 World's Fair. So I went over to Westmoreland, Portland, Kingsbury, and Westminster—Anglophile names that showed off the city's Eastern aspirations but betrayed its French and German heritage. I would make most of my revenues from the maids who would give me a couple of dollars just to go away. But I could also knock on more doors in less time if I ventured into a small hotel, like the brick Town House Hotel on Pershing Avenue.

On the other side of the state, shortly after 11 a.m. on September 28, 1953, a taxi from the Toedman Cab Company in Kansas City had pulled up in front of the French Institute of Notre Dame de Sion, a brick Catholic elementary school near downtown. A short, stout woman got out and labored up the steps to the double front doors. It was stiflingly hot—it would reach 103°F before the day was over—but she was dressed primly in a beige nylon blouse, dark skirt, white gloves, and a brown hat over her reddish-brown hair. When the door attendant, Sister Morand, answered, the woman—clearly distraught—identified herself as the sister of Virginia Greenlease, the mother of a wealthy student at the school, Bobby Greenlease. The woman said that Bobby's mother had suffered a heart attack while shopping at the fashionable Country Club Plaza on the south side of town. She was now at St. Mary's Hospital and was asking to see her six-year-old son. Could Bobby be taken from school to visit his mother in the hospital?

Bobby was upstairs in his first-grade Latin class. Sister Morand said she would fetch him. She then asked the visitor if she would like to pray for Bobby's mother in the chapel while she waited. "I'm not a Catholic," the woman said. "I don't know if God will answer my prayers." But she entered the chapel and knelt in prayer. A few minutes later, Sister returned with Bobby, who was proudly wearing a Jerusalem cross that he'd won in class, pinned with a red ribbon to his shirt. The FBI summary report later noted that Sister Morand recalled that Bobby walked directly to the woman without hesitation and there was nothing in his action or behavior to indicate doubt on his part that this woman was his aunt. As the woman left the school, she had an arm around Bobby's shoulder and was holding his hand. "There was nothing about this to make us suspicious," said one of the nuns later. "One does not look for trouble." But then she added, "The world is much closer to falling apart than we sometimes realize."[7]

A half hour later, another nun, anxious about the heart attack episode, called the Greenlease home to check on the mother's condition. Virginia Greenlease herself came to the phone. "Why, I'm fine," she said. "Why are you asking? Is something the matter?"

As the taxi pulled away from Bobby's school, the driver, Willard P. Creech, heard the woman peppering the boy with questions: "What are the names of your dogs? What is the name of your parrot?" Bobby cheerfully replied to her questions. As the FBI report put it, "He seemed to be a happy bright little boy who just thought he was going for a ride." In a few minutes, the cab pulled up at the parking lot by the Katz drugstore at 40th and Main. There, waiting in Plymouth station wagon, was a pale, sallow-faced man in a blue sharkskin suit, size 42. "Hello, Bobby," he said. "How are you?" Bobby climbed into the front seat between the man and the woman who had picked him up at school. In the back of the car was a dog, a boxer named Doc.

The first note from the kidnappers arrived a few hours later. It had been sent special delivery, postmarked at 6 p.m. It bore the wrong address for the Greenleases' home in the well-to-do neighborhood of Mission Hills—but the police had already alerted the post office to be on the lookout for it. The note, with its unnerving misspellings, read:

> Your boy been kiddnapped get $600,000 in $20's–$10's–Fed. Res. notes from all twelve districts we realize it takes a few days to get that amount. Boy will be in good hands—when you have money ready put ad in K.C. Star. M—will meet you in Chicago next Sunday–signed Mr. G.
>
> Do not call police or try to use chemicals on bills or take numbers. Do not try to use any radio to catch us or boy dies. If you try to trap us your wife and your other child and yourself will be killed you will be watched all of the time. You will be told later how to contact us with money. When you get this note let us know by driving up and down main St. between 39 & 29 for twenty minutes with white rag on car aeriel.
>
> Over

On the other side was written:

If do exactly as we say an try no tricks, your boy will be back safe within 24 hrs afer we check money.

Deliver money in army duefel bag. Be ready to deliver at once on contact.

M.

$400,000 in 20's

$200,000 in 10's

The kidnappers were asking for a staggering ransom—in today's terms, more than $5 million. But the seventy-one-year-old Robert Greenlease did not hesitate. Bobby was his precious third child; he had an older son, Paul, by his first marriage, which had ended in divorce. With his younger second wife, he had a daughter, Virginia Sue, and then Robert Cosgrove Greenlease Jr., the bright-eyed boy everyone called Bobby. Greenlease told the police and FBI to keep their distance; he and a few trusted friends would fulfill the kidnappers' demands and get Bobby home safely.[8]

Kidnapping is rare in the United States, then and now, and it compels public attention like no other crime. Twenty years had passed since the abduction and murder of Charles Lindbergh's son in 1932. But even the Lindbergh kidnapping predated the hothouse atmospherics generated by television. With the Greenlease case, the new nightly TV newscasts could broadcast every frightening detail into every home, real time.

In 1952, the FCC had lifted the freeze on new station licenses, and the number of TV stations mushroomed from 108 in 65 cities in 1952 to 198 in 241 cities a year later. As a result, the reach of TV news had spread enormously, both locally and nationally. CBS offered a fifteen-minute national news broadcast, *Douglas Edwards with the News*, and made Walter Cronkite famous at the 1952 national political conventions. NBC had the

Camel News Caravan with John Cameron Swayze and a fortune in tobacco money behind it. Both networks had begun shooting their own film reports, rather than relying on syndicated newsreel services.

This was the fifties, the prelapsarian fifties, not the fantasy decade that popular culture handed to us in *Leave It to Beaver* and *Father Knows Best.* If the box in the corner did not change all American households, it certainly changed the way we think about them. Human lives and news events after 1953 have been presented and interpreted by the mass media. The rough edges were rubbed smooth. As a result, the experienced world of 1953 remains almost unknowably *strange*, as remote as the Middle Ages. When we try to make sense of that year, the pieces do not fit easily into a seamless narrative. Yet the events unfolding then have more to do with the asymmetric America of today than anything else we know.

The Greenlease kidnapping was in fact the first major crime to achieve national prominence in the age of television; we had not yet learned how to process crime news of this intensity and intimacy. It's hard to overstate the fascination that the Greenlease kidnapping engendered among little kids then. Bobby himself was a leading-edge baby boomer, one of the first unfortunately designated celebrities of his generation. The Greenleases were one of the richest and most prominent families in Kansas City. Robert Greenlease Sr. was a millionaire who owned General Motors car dealerships all across the Great Plains. But now, like the Lindberghs in 1932, they were left alone to deal with the media in their sorrow.

On Wednesday morning, the Greenleases received another special-delivery letter. Like the first, it was handwritten. This one repeated the original instructions and added: "Boy is ok but homesick don't try to stop us on pick up or boy dies." Afterwards, the obviously distressed Robert Greenlease came outside to talk to the press but could only haltingly say, "I think the kidnappers are trying to contact us," before collapsing into sobs.

In truth, Bobby was already dead, shot and killed by an alcoholic ex-convict named Carl Austin Hall. Hall and his accomplice, Bonnie Brown Heady, a sex worker, had buried Bobby in her backyard in St. Joseph, Missouri. After collecting the ransom of $600,000 in cash stuffed into a duffel bag, they fled to St. Louis.

On Tuesday, October 6—the day after the New York Yankees won their fifth straight World Series with a 4–3 victory over the Brooklyn Dodgers at Yankee Stadium—I somehow got inside the Town House, an annex of the Congress Hotel on Union Boulevard. I wandered up and down the hotel corridors, knocking on room doors, trying to sell tickets to the Boy Scout circus. What I did not know was that on that same day, sitting in Room 324 in the Town House, was Carl Hall, drinking bourbon and shooting morphine, armed with the same .38 caliber Smith and Wesson snub-nose revolver he had used to kill Bobby Greenlease. Later that night, he was arrested by St. Louis police who had been tipped off by his cab driver.

Just eighty-one days later, Carl and Bonnie had been tried and executed in Missouri—the swiftest such punishment at that time. They were tried under the "Lindbergh law," which provided for the death penalty for kidnappers. Only $300,000 of the ransom was recovered; the rest fell into the hands of corrupt police and local gangsters.

In its editorial on the verdicts, the *New York Times* wrote, "There never seems much point after the deed is done to speak out vindictive strictures against so heinous, so contrary to all human feeling, that no punishment the civilized laws of this land allow seems quite adequate."[9]

The Lindberghs would have agreed. Celebrities were not safe.

The twentieth-century figure who most rivaled Charles Lindbergh in a precipitous rise to fame was Albert Einstein. But while it took Lindbergh thirty-three hours and thirty minutes—the time of his transatlantic flight—to achieve world-wide acclaim, Einstein did it in just six minutes and fifty-one seconds—the amount of time that the moon floated across the face of the sun in an eclipse on May 29, 1919.

Arthur Eddington, a member of the British Royal Astro-nomical Society, had sailed to the remote island of Príncipe, off the African coast, to measure the bending of starlight made by the sun there. The measurements confirmed Einstein's 1915 the-ory of general relativity. The public announcement was made November 6, 1919, by J. J. Thomson, president of the society, who proclaimed it "one of the greatest achievements of human thought."[10]

The world was astonished. Newspapers proclaimed that Ein-stein had overturned Newton and Euclid and had "destroyed space and time." On November 10, the *New York Times* splashed the headline "Lights All Askew in the Heavens; Men of Science More or Less Agog by the Eclipse Measurements; Stars Not Near Where They Seemed or Were Calculated to Be, but No-body Need Worry."

Einstein was already a famous scientist for his papers on rel-ativity in 1905 and 1915. But now, in sharp contrast to Galileo, he was the first celebrity of science to be hailed as such while alive. Six hundred articles and books appeared in six years, and a book-length biography in two years. The philosopher Marshall Missner argues that the particular timing made the burst of ce-lebrity almost inevitable. Still soon after the First World War, much of the Western world was xenophobic and anti-Semitic. That alone would bring attention to this mysterious Jewish pac-ifist, much of it unwanted.[11]

Everything changed again when Einstein traveled to America in 1921 as part of a Zionist delegation led by Chaim Weizmann. Einstein's mission was to advance the cause of Zionism, but he was covered enthusiastically by both the Yiddish- and English-language press. He was something new under the sun. He was not an austere and unapproachable

European scientist but rather a grandfatherly Jewish sage of modesty and humility, with a twinkle in his eye. He was full of wit and quotable aphorisms. After his first lectures at Princeton University, he answered a question by quipping, "Subtle is the Lord, but malicious he is not"—which just convinced the multitudes that he was a secular saint.[12]

Einstein repeatedly complained about his status as a celebrity, a term which itself produced more annoyance than pride. He felt "hounded by the press and other riff-raff," he wrote to his friend Max Born. "It's so dreadful that I can barely breathe anymore, not to mention getting around to any sensible work." To Ludwig Hopf, he confessed, "Since the flood of newspaper articles, I've been so deluged with questions, invitations, and requests that I dream I'm burning in Hell and the postman is the Devil eternally roaring at me, hurling new bundles of letters at my head because I have not yet answered the old ones."[13]

The reporters were smitten with the idea that Einstein was an otherworldly genius in a land of mortals. Reporting a probably apocryphal incident, the *Manchester Guardian* claimed, "When he offered his last important work to the publishers, he warned them there were not more than twelve persons in the whole world who understood it. Nevertheless, they took the risk."[14] When he heard this tale, Einstein laughed and denied it. But that didn't stop the *Washington Post* from repeating it when he arrived in America.

As Walter Isaacson explains in his insightful biography of Einstein, "Einstein's response to adulation was as complex as that of cosmos to gravity. He was attracted and repelled by the cameras, loved publicity and loved to complain about it. His love-hate relationship with fame and reporters might seem unusual until one reflects on how similar it was to the mix of enjoyment, amusement, aversion, and annoyance that so many other famous people have felt."[15]

American commercialism eagerly acted as what the scholar Richard Crockatt calls "a multiplier on his public impact."[16] By the time he moved to Princeton, New Jersey, in 1933 to join the faculty at the Institute for Advanced Study, his appearance had become almost cartoonishly recognizable—the shock of unruly white hair, the pipe, the sweatshirts, no socks—all ready to be branded. He was something new, the celebrity-ready scientist, a phrase that was no longer oxymoronic. The image of Einstein was one of the mass media's characteristic products, ready to be reproduced and refined and reshaped over the years like any other image generated by celebrity culture. Despite his often-voiced antipathy toward publicity, he and his wife, Elsa, still appeared on the red carpet in 1931 for the Los Angeles premiere of Charlie Chaplin's *City Lights.*

Einstein's irreverence, which often bordered on the characteristic defiance displayed by celebrities, could get him into trouble. A conversation he had with the niece of a Dutch colleague published by a Dutch newspaper caused an uproar when reprinted in the *New York Times* and many other newspapers. In it, Einstein complained about the level of boredom and spiritual poverty in American society that made people susceptible to fads and empty pleasures. American men, he said, "are toy dogs for their wives, who spend the money in the most excessive fashion and who shroud themselves in a veil of extravagance." Worse, he made fun of the "Einstein-craze" as a result of the "magic of incomprehension." Afterwards, Einstein moved quickly to explain and disown many of his remarks. He had learned a hard lesson about the public impact of a celebrity's words.[17]

Einstein did not curtail his pacifist views though. He had opposed the First World War and cultivated friendships with a who's who of twentieth-century public intellectuals—Gandhi, Albert Schweitzer, Bertrand Russell, George Bernard Shaw, H. G. Wells, Thomas Mann, and John Dewey. In America, he embraced civil rights causes and befriended the Black Americans behind them. When the Black opera singer Marian Anderson gave a concert in Princeton in 1937 but was denied a room at the Nassau Inn, Einstein invited her to stay at his house, which she did and returned to several more times, including two months before he died. Einstein's war against racism also extended to defending the Scottsboro Boys and to his twenty-year friendship with the actor-activist Paul Robeson, who had grown up in Princeton.

Among the ironies of history is that Einstein once crossed paths with his only peer as a contemporary celebrity, Charles Lindbergh. In 1939, after Einstein and the physicist Leo Szilard had drafted their famous letter to President Franklin Roosevelt about the dangers of the Nazi development of an atomic bomb, they debated who should deliver the letter to Roosevelt. Einstein had met Lindbergh a few years earlier, so, aware of Lindbergh's popularity but unaware of Lindbergh's isolationism, he wrote a cover letter for Szilard. "I would like to ask you to do me a favor of receiving my friend Dr. Szilard and think very carefully about what he will tell you," Einstein wrote to Lindbergh. "To one who is outside of science the matter he will bring up may seem fantastic. However, you will certainly become convinced that a possibility is presented here which has to be very carefully watched in the public interest."[18]

Lindbergh never replied, and a few months later he delivered a nationwide radio address for isolationism with hints of pro-German sentiments and anti-Semitism. Einstein and Szilard decided Lindbergh was not their emissary after all. They eventually gave the letter to Alexander Sachs, an economist and friend of Roosevelt. The result was the Manhattan Project.

CHAPTER 4

WHEN BIG NAMES DID GOOD WORKS

The first shift in twentieth-century celebrity came when the images moved from print and newspapers to the movies. In the Golden Age of Hollywood, as the studios liked to call it, the stars were glamorized—usually within the context of the roles they played. In real life, they were considered unapproachable, but, according to the studios' publicity apparatus, if we were lucky enough to see them off-screen, we would see that they were regular people like us—who happened to be talented and deserving. What we did not see was the selective way the studio system chose to micromanage their human products. Black people and other people of color were kept on the other side of the velvet rope.

If there is a single celebrity whose life encompassed the twists and turns of the star system in the twentieth century, it was Elizabeth Taylor. A movie star by the time she was twelve years old and starred in the 1944 film classic *National Velvet*, Taylor grew up as a creature of the once-dominant Hollywood studio system, winning two Oscars along the way. But she balked at giving all control to the studio, and headlines about her private life soon dominated her professional life.

At a time that enshrined suburbanite tranquility, Taylor fit the celebrity pattern of a defiant outlier, a glamorous movie star who kicked off feeding frenzies in the media with her sensational affairs and eight marriages to seven different men, including actors Eddie Fisher and Richard Burton (twice). But then, gossip generated gold, and in 1960, 20th Century-Fox paid her an unheard-of $1 million to make *Cleopatra* with Richard Burton, making her the highest-paid movie star ever.

The tabloids and the movie magazines feasted on Liz 'n' Dick. When an Italian photographer named Marcello Geppetti used a telephoto lens to photograph Taylor and Burton embracing on the deck of a yacht in the Mediterranean in 1962, it redefined the relationship between the public lives and private lives of movie stars. The Geppetti photos and the movie *La Dolce Vita* introduced the word *paparazzi* to the media environment. They were soon followed by Ron Galella's pursuit of Jacqueline Onassis and many others. When Andy Warhol created his famous 1963 silkscreen *Liz*, she had become, like his soup can, an icon of mass culture.

Ironically, the paparazzi photos of Taylor and Burton are an eerie preview of the photos taken thirty-five years later of Princess Diana and her lover, Dodi Fayed, also on a yacht in the Mediterranean. Not long after Taylor and Burton were photographed on the yacht, they were besieged in Boston by mobs of fans and paparazzi when Burton performed in *Hamlet* there. The parallels fatefully continued when paparazzi, similarly pursuing Diana, contributed to her fatal automobile accident in Paris in 1997.

In the second half of her life, Elizabeth Taylor stopped making movies and became the world's first purebred celebrity. She curated her personal life for the media as assiduously as earlier stars had done for their professional lives. Fan magazines like *Photoplay* and *Modern Screen* followed her escapades avidly. When the startup called *People* needed a cover subject for its first test issue in 1973, the face on the cover was Elizabeth

Taylor's. Ever defiant, Taylor monetized her reputation into a brand, putting her name on a line of jewelry and an array of fragrances including Elizabeth Taylor's Passion, White Diamonds, and Black Pearls. It is a business model still emulated today by the likes of Paris Hilton, Gwyneth Paltrow, and Ariana Grande.

She also was no longer the flirty playgirl portrayed in the Liz 'n Dick tabloid covers. I found this out in the fall of 1990 when I interviewed Taylor for *People*.[1] This was a transaction negotiated with her longtime publicist Chen Sam that offered benefits to everyone. *People* gained an exclusive story that would potentially reap millions in newsstand sales. She gained the prospect of publicity for her House of Taylor cosmetic brands and her chosen cause of pediatric AIDS.

Looking back on that interview, I once again recalled Rudolf Otto's idea of "numinosity" from *The Idea of the Holy*. For me, though, the feeling of awe was generated not by a goddess but rather by a celebrity. When she unexpectedly greeted me in person at the door of her brick-and-shingle house in Los Angeles's Bel Air enclave, I was so rattled I dropped my gift bouquet of lavender flowers, along with two portable tape recorders, with a resounding crash on the floor.

Inside, sunlight streamed through fingertip-high windows into a living room that was as informal as one can get that has a Frans Hals portrait over the fireplace. Elsewhere the walls glowed with fine oils by master painters—a Rouault, a Pissarro —a collection that reflected Elizabeth's upscale upbringing as the daughter of a London art dealer. A needlepoint pillow on a chair stated a credo, "IT'S NOT THE HAVING, IT'S THE GET-TING," which its owner had lived up to on both counts.

At home, the woman who rode a horse to fame forty-six years earlier in *National Velvet* was still surrounded by animals. There was Nellie, the collie that Charles Bronson had presented to her the previous year for her charitable work, and there was Max, a baby parrot she hand-fed. Max's predecessor in parrot-hood,

Alvin, lived with Elizabeth for ten years before he died. In her store appearance promotions for Passion, Elizabeth delighted customers by turning on her Maggie the Cat Southern accent borrowed from one of her most famous film roles, as the manipulative wife in *Cat on a Hot Tin Roof.* She then described Alvin as "my main man, my little green man, and for three years the only man who has been privy to my bedroom."

In his last two years, though, Alvin was sharing at least some room with Larry Fortensky, the former construction worker Elizabeth met at the Betty Ford Center in 1988. Fortensky is the man who supported Taylor faithfully in her efforts to cleanse herself of pills and alcohol.

Her pride in her sobriety explained the $20 million lawsuit she directed at the *National Enquirer* after it claimed that she was drinking in the hospital:

> They went a little too far, and I finally got sick of it. They went into long, laborious detail about how I'd been drunk in the hospital, and the doctors had me on a suicide watch, and all this rubbish. This was completely untrue. It hurt me, and it has hurt others who believed in me. I received thousands of letters from people who said, "We've looked up to you. How could you?" I felt betrayed, and I felt I was betraying others. People kept saying, "Well, why don't you sue?" So finally I did—not for the money, but really for the principle of it.

Taylor had identified the sore spot in the usual symbiosis between celebrities and the press. After her would come a parade of celebrity litigants, ranging from Sarah Palin to Meghan Markle.

The same sense of indignation made Taylor a genuine heroine in the battle against AIDS. Her involvement with the American Foundation for AIDS Research (amfAR) began in 1984 when she was asked to host the first AIDS fundraising dinner ever. She then ran into "seven months of absolute and abject rejection" before finding supporters. "I thought, 'This is unbelievable what is going on. People aren't aware of the problem because of the stigma.' And I personally was very aware of the stigma because of the reaction people were giving me."

When her friend, the leading man Rock Hudson, later became sick, she explained, "I was already involved in it before any of us knew what was the matter with Rock. Then, of course, I found out and visited him. When I spoke with his doctors, I learned more and more about the disease. And that just made me angry. It was my anger that involved me with AIDS, and it still is. Nobody asks for this disease. Nobody deserves it. We're all as innocent as babies in the eyes of God."

Motivated by personal friendships and feelings of empathy toward all gay people—not a widespread public sentiment then—Elizabeth went to work. Dr. Mathilde Krim, the biologist and with Elizabeth the founding co-chair of amfAR, credits Taylor with helping bring AIDS awareness into the American mainstream. "At the time, very few people were willing to speak up publicly for this cause," she says. "Elizabeth said she wanted to be head of it."[2]

Taylor's escort to the 1989 World AIDS Day fundraiser was her friend Malcolm Forbes, who had already given her a $1 million check for amfAR. His death just a few months later left her grieving. "I loved him. He loved me," she said firmly. "I miss him enormously. He knew how to give joy, and he loved to share. He was the least stingy soul I've ever met."

She felt a different sadness about the death of her designer friend Roy Halston Frowick, known as Halston, from AIDS. "I didn't know until the last year. We all thought it was something else. So many people who are sick with AIDS don't want people to know because of the stigma involved. And that's sad. They're not allowed the dignity afforded someone who is dying. How dare we take that away from anyone?"

In Hollywood's Golden Age, a few other stars similarly took on pro bono causes—Jerry Lewis (muscular dystrophy), Danny

Thomas (pediatric cancer), and Jane Fonda (social activism). But the path of virtue was not always clearly marked.

In the monocultures of the 1950s and early 1960s, the public viewed Elizabeth Taylor's life as a cautionary tale. The fan magazines exploited the public's fascination with her misbehavior, drug abuse, and very public divorces in cover after cover. She was often ridiculed.

But in her defiance, Taylor was not so different from Sarah Bernhardt or Calamity Jane. She could separate herself from her public persona, gain control over her life, and still had the clout to monetize her fame.

"When I first started doing the work I did for AIDS," she said in 1990, "it was very unpopular. A lot of people told me I'd be badly burned by it, that it was very undignified. And I didn't give a hoot what people thought about it then, and I don't now. It's just that there has to be something done about it. I want to do all I can because I have to live with me."

The woman I met that day was the opposite of a vacuous celebrity. She was serious and self-aware and had a sense of humor. She embodied the redemption narrative in that she had successfully conquered her drug abuse and found a larger cause to devote herself to—and redeemed herself.

If anything, Elizabeth Taylor had outlived the studio system. Others like Marilyn Monroe did not. The arrival of serialized network television brought the second explosion in images and impact—but downward mobility for celebrities. Now it was less of a glamorous Hollywood royalty than a turbulent, ever-changing world of Archie and Edith Bunker. Archie Bunker was such a beloved and watchable character in part because he was so recognizable. Many families (especially many white families) had someone in it who looked and spoke like Archie Bunker.

It would be a short step from Archie and Edith Bunker to the world of reality television and the Kardashians. Becoming a celebrity was not an achievement but rather a condition—the condition of being talked about. One way to define a celebrity is that you become one when the public is as interested in your private life as in your professional role. Confining public attention to accounts of someone's professional life had previously been our approach to the famous.

As *People* discovered, devoting attention to a prominent person's private life erases our differences: everyone eats breakfast, exercises, fights with those they love. When the public began to shift its gaze from the glamorous likes of Marilyn Monroe and Elizabeth Taylor, it was also shifting its taste from the extraordinary to the ordinary, from the godlike stars to Archie Bunker, whose quotidian life Americans strangely began to find just as intriguing.

Elizabeth Taylor found her redemption in conquering her personal flaws—and then devoting herself to good works. This pattern appeared to reach its apogee in the life of Princess Diana of England. She was a holdover from the glamorous days of celebrity who woke up blinking in the hot glare of tabloid fame. The soap opera saga of her courtship, marriage, and then separation from Prince Charles generated more covers than any celebrity, before or since. As of 2022, she had appeared on *People's* cover a total of fifty-eight times. Why? Because her life could be distilled into one rule for success that captured a primary principle of celebrity journalism: "Write about a woman with a problem."

So we did.

K ensington Palace, please."
The sky was a pearly Ascot gray on a cool Tuesday morning in October 1994 as the London bureau chief of *People,* Fred Hauptfuhrer, and I scrambled into a red compact taxi. After one wrong turn—the driver thought we meant Kensington Park, not Palace—we were waved past a gatehouse and into the grounds of the three-hundred-year-old brick edifice where Queen Victoria was born and the Princess of Wales then lived.

It is still hard to assess the celebrity apotheosis that Diana represented in 1994. During her compressed life—she was only thirty-six when she died—she was the most famous woman in the world. During her fraught marriage with Prince Charles (they were by then separated), celebrity gossip had been weaponized. Unwillingly or not, she was as much a part of the celebrity-industrial complex as Elizabeth Taylor.

These circumstances would return to the public square with the controversies surrounding the Netflix series *The Crown*, which would prove a blockbuster TV series from its first season in 2016 through its fifth, in 2022–23. Was it a "hatchet job," as the former royal press secretary Dickie Arbiter has charged? Or was it something like the truth, if not fully accurate? In either case, what prevailed from the emergence of Shy Di until the twenty-first century was the public's ever-ravenous appetite for gossip about the royal family.

In our 1994 visit, we were welcomed inside the palace by a butler dressed in a coat and tie—presumably her longtime confidant Paul Burrell—who ushered us into an anteroom with chartreuse wallpaper. The feeling was suburban and homey, not heraldic—more East Hampton than Hampton Court. The butler gestured toward an open door and suddenly Diana appeared, extending her hand with a laugh, almost a giggle. I greeted her with "How are you?," completely forgetting my careful instructions that the only two proper ways to greet the princess were as "Your Highness" or "Ma'am."

I was there to broach with Diana the idea that she might participate in a charity fundraiser sponsored by *People*. It was a partnership that could be mutually beneficial. We would take advantage of her celebrity magnetism. She could take advantage of the publicity and benefits we brought to her chosen causes: the Elizabeth Glaser Pediatric AIDS Foundation and the Royal Marsden Hospital, specializing in cancer treatment, in London. The result would be her fulfilling the "generativity" phase—acting to help future generations—that is at the end of the redemption cycle so familiar among celebrities.

The three of us sat on facing green-and-white chintz sofas—Fred and I on one, Diana on another; embroidered scarlet throw pillows were scattered about. Diana was open, spontaneous, and not at all guarded. She laughed freely and gaily, usually at something she said—not surprisingly, since we were utterly focused, nervous, and humorless throughout.

She had a beguiling habit of clapping her hands on her face or crossing them on her chest if something amused her or if she was laughing at herself. If it is possible to be both professional and flirtatious, she was. When there was a pause in the conversation—usually while we were either desperately trying to think of our next question or interrupting one another—she would sit in the pose familiar from her photos: legs folded together at a sharp angle, hands in lap, eyes slightly downcast. Her visual appearance was of girlishness and shyness, but her personality was outgoing and confident.

She seemed to be the image *People* described in its first words written about her in 1981: "Think of her as the Girl Next Door, a blue-eyed blonde with a peaches and Devonshire cream complexion."

Before and during the time of our visit, the Fleet Street tabloids had erupted in one of their periodic feeding frenzies over the dissolution of Diana's marriage to Prince Charles. We asked her how she was coping with the onslaught of publicity. She said that she tried to ignore it but was concerned about "its impact on William and Harry."

The princess then said that she had concluded that one way to deal with her problems with the press was to get to know it better, so she was having small meetings with editors. (By implication, our tea was part of this strategy.) She said that she had recently met with "Mr. Murdoch," whose tabloids had been among the most virulent in reporting on her private life.

Diana told us that she was willing to collaborate on a charity event for pediatric AIDS in the US. As the conversation began to lag, we put down our coffee cups and rose to leave. She walked us downstairs, thanking me for taking time to see her during my visit to London. (Not an inconvenience at all, I assured her.)

The fruits of our labor would come in June 1996. Henry Bienen, Northwestern University's president, whom I had known since he was dean of Princeton's then Woodrow Wilson School, and I escorted the princess to a gala in Chicago, where we shared an intimate dinner with 1,500 guests who paid up to $35,000 a table to join us.

The princess was charming, witty, charismatic, compassionate, and totally professional. The palace said I could have the first dance with her, provided I met three conditions. First, I had to be a good dancer. *Check!* Second, I had to be happily married. *Check!* Third, I had to be six feet tall. *Oh well.* In the end, we raised $1.4 million for the charities.

If Diana had lived, today she would be more than sixty years old and a grandmother of five. She would not have gone the society route of the Duke and Duchess of Windsor. Her model more likely would have been Elizabeth Taylor and her array of charitable causes. Would she enjoy *The Crown?* Or would she see in it a metaphor for her famous cause to remove land mines around the world?

Life is a minefield.

Once outside that day in Kensington Palace, we stood for a few minutes by the car, chatting about the weather, of all things. As we pulled out of the driveway, I turned to look back and saw what will remain my lasting image of her: the Princess of Wales standing by her doorway, alone, plaintively waving goodbye.[3]

CHAPTER 5

SEX, LIES, AND SOCIAL MEDIA

There is too much democracy in the culture, and not enough in the society." So lamented the writer and social commentator Fran Lebowitz talking about the celebrity-manufacturing machine that started with P. T. Barnum and his human exhibits and then took us to Lindbergh, Hollywood, reality television, and the Kardashians.[1]

Indeed, she has a point. Such has been the power of social media to inflict celebrities on us that even Hollywood, that most aristocratic of American institutions, lost control and had to open its gates to "stars" whose primary skill isn't entertainment, but rather, the cultivation of fame. Faced with this new breed of celebrity, all the stars in Hollywood's traditional firmament followed suit, using Facebook, Twitter, TikTok, and Instagram to feed it any clickbait at hand to engage often the basest passions of audiences.

What arrived first, though, was what would become the one breeding ground of celebrity culture almost everyone agrees to hate: reality television. In no other pocket of widening celebrity is the banality of its attainment so explicitly on display. But the origins of the genre were far nobler. In the early 1970s, the Loud family of Santa Barbara paved the way with a public television documentary program called *An American Family*. Over twelve one-hour episodes, the first-ever reality show chronicled the daily life of an upper-middle-class family as they struggled with marital issues, economic problems, and a misunderstood gay son. Viewers followed their evolving family realities on television once a week. The show was produced during a time of national uncertainty following the Vietnam War and captured in Don McLean's melancholy number-one hit, "American Pie." The earnest approach taken by the PBS documentary was intended to provide insights to parents of baby boomers living on the cusp of social change.

Lance Loud is thought to be the first openly gay character on TV. Watching his parents' divorce might have been helpful to families struggling with similar issues. But the impact included launching a genre that became a form of entertainment kudzu that was far more voyeuristic than intended. Not surprisingly, the Louds were billed on the first cover of *People*.

There have now been at least a hundred different types of reality television shows produced over the years: young adulthood (*The Real World*), dating (*The Bachelor*), documentary style (*Keeping Up with the Kardashians*), talent contests (*American Idol*), law enforcement (*COPS*), makeover (*How Clean Is Your House?*), lifestyle (*Queer Eye*), adventure (*Survivor*), and many others.

All of these shows generate overnight celebrities. There are no longer a handful of media gatekeepers deciding who will be made famous, and there is no longer a small universe of agreed-upon celebrities. As Fran Lebowitz pointed out, the process has been democratized—anyone can become famous with enough audacity, patience, and Twitter followers. On one hand, this potentially opens the halls of celebrity to previously marginalized people of color and different body types, for example. On the other hand, fame can become the goal, not the reward. The greater the number of media outlets, the less individuals must do to achieve renown. They just have to attract eyeballs, which in turn attract advertisers and generate profits.

What came after reality television? The rise of the internet and social media and the new generation of celebrities they created.

It began with the received wisdom that the first category to profit from any new media technology is pornography—from moveable type to daguerreotypes to film and videotapes. The second is celebrity.

Like her prototype, the singer and actress Josephine Baker, Paris Hilton entered the public arena as a model and socialite who liked to party. She was called New York's leading "It Girl" and made cameo appearances in movies like *Zoolander* and Vincent Gallo's "Honey Bunny" video. In 2002, she played a lead role in the straight-to-video horror film *Nine Lives*.

Hilton might still have been a little-known party girl, but everything changed in December 2003 when her then boyfriend Rick Salomon leaked their two-year-old sex tape online and later sold it to a porn website under the title *1 Night in Paris*. Soon thereafter, Hilton and her friend Nicole Richie attracted thirteen million viewers with their own reality show, *The Simple Life*. In just over a year, Hilton released a *New York Times* best-selling autobiography, introduced her own lifestyle brand, hosted *Saturday Night Live* (February 2005), starred in the major horror film *House of Wax* (2005), and published her second best-selling book, *Your Heiress Diary: Confess It All to Me* (2005).

Which brings us to the Kardashians and yet another career-launching sex tape.

In March 2007, Kim Kardashian was an unknown stylist for Paris Hilton. But then her own sex tape, recorded in 2003 with her then-boyfriend William "Ray J" Norwood, was "leaked" into the public domain. In his book *Kardashian Dynasty*, Ian Halperin argues that the tape was intentionally devised to bring

Kardashian fame. He quotes a source who alleges that a mutual friend of Kim and Paris's had advised Kim that "if she wanted to achieve fame, a sex tape would be the way to go and helped her put the video together." Further, according to Halperin, "the source claimed that Kim had discussed the idea of producing a tape with her family beforehand."[2] Both Kim and Kris Kardashian have repeatedly denied this story over the years. In 2007, Kardashian filed a lawsuit against Vivid Entertainment and received help from Joe Francis, the creator of *Girls Gone Wild*, to acquire the rights to the video for $4.5 million.[3]

It was Kim's mother, Kris Jenner, who, in 2006, came up with the idea for a reality show about the Kardashian-Jenners and took it to co-producer Ryan Seacrest and the E! network. The result was twenty seasons of a genre-breaking reality show, as well as countless TV specials and spin-offs, books, fragrances, apparel and accessory lines, a string of boutiques, and endless critical sneers.[4] KimKardashian.com is the world's most popular official celebrity website, according to its host service.[5] The name *Kardashian* has become synonymous with celebrity branding.

What do we see here?

First, that by flouting normally accepted standards of behavior, Paris Hilton and Kim Kardashian were in the tradition of the defiant celebrity, whose ancestry traces to Calamity Jane, Oscar Wilde, Sarah Bernhardt, and Malcolm X. The difference is that the newest defiant celebrities owe their visibility to publicity and nudity alone, not ability or talent, not even faked ability.

Second, that celebrities create and encourage consumption at every level. We watch what they do and want to own what they own. The more that media technology has expanded, the easier it has become for celebrities to become more famous, develop their brands, and encourage more consumption. The result is the symbiotic triad still with us: celebrities, media, and marketing.

The marriage of social media with celebrity culture was made in branding heaven. Just as the broad reach of television had once overshadowed the traditional legacy print media, so too did social media offer unparalleled reach, frequency, and intimacy, especially to younger tween consumers. The pioneering platform was the now-forgotten SixDegrees in 1997, followed soon by Friendster and MySpace in 2003, Facebook and Flickr in 2004, then YouTube in 2005, Twitter in 2006, Instagram in 2010, Snapchat in 2011, and TikTok in 2016. With its 2.9 billion active users every month, Facebook/Meta is now the world's largest social network.[6]

Third, the Kardashians demonstrated that public contempt is not a career killer as long as the same people who profess to despise you continue to talk about you. Are you listening, Donald Trump?

Soon a new generation of celebrities used social media to bypass reality television and the traditional star-making machinery altogether. For their brands, celebrities were now operating at a scale that was impossible to ignore. The stars were generating not only sales of the products but also producing reams of demographic details about their followers that could be exploited endlessly.

Here are some of the pioneering social influencers in—what else?—boldface names.

Colbie Caillat had been rejected in an early round of *American Idol* and never made it before the judges. She had never heard of social media, she explained to the *Washington Post* in 2007. "I never really understood the whole thing, thought it was really weird," she said. "Then one of my good friends said people make *music* pages on MySpace where other people can hear your music. He created the page and uploaded my song and showed me how to use it, and one day I started getting friends on there, started getting responses to the music."[7]

Dozens of her friends became hundreds, became thousands. In October, soon after Caillat passed the six-thousand-friend mark, *Rolling Stone* hailed her as one of the music scene's most promising unsigned artists. She stayed long enough, though, to be the number-one unsigned artist on MySpace for four successive months, during which Caillat gathered ten million plays and kept signing up friends. The total surpassed 166,000 followers, with total plays of more than sixteen million. Caillat signed with Universal in March 2007. The numbers remained impressive after Caillat's debut album was released July 2007. Within hours of its release, *Coco* debuted at number one on iTunes' albums chart. By the time she signed with the Creative Artists Agency (CAA), in 2021, Caillat had sold over six million albums worldwide and over ten million singles.[8]

Other unknowns have used social media to boost their recognition before moving on to more traditional categories of celebrity. In April 2011, the model **Kate Upton** and her friends posted a video on YouTube of her doing a hip-hop dance at a Los Angeles Clippers basketball game. It went viral. Guy Trebay of the *New York Times* observed that this served to illustrate the power of social media to bestow stardom upon a model, thereby bypassing the traditional launching pad of the top designer runway shows.[9]

In April 2012, Upton appeared in a video of herself performing the "Cat Daddy" dance to the song of the same name by The Rej3ctz, which also went viral. Upton had some modest modelling success before these events (she had a photo on the cover of the *Sports Illustrated* swimsuit issue and had been the face of Guess lingerie). But she wasn't yet successful at getting her name in boldface type. Then Upton joined Twitter in October 2010 and, as of October 2022, had 2.1 million followers.

If the celebrities who are created by social media have one thing in common, it is their insistence that they are distinguished by their everyday qualities. When asked to explain her rise to fame, Upton noted, "What can I say? I'm relatable."

This suggests that the fashionable gloss that was for so long the sign that a celebrity had made it and that for so long made them desirable no longer has the same appeal that it once did.

Executives are now creating celebrities—think pop singer Ed Sheeran—who seem to look like us, who wear regular clothes, who aren't extremely attractive—people with whom we can identify. It's the capacity of the star to conjure this just-folks feeling in fans that marketers are now looking for and often have delivered to fans who scroll through their smartphones looking for a sense of relatability.

The mark of a celebrity who became famous before the social media wave, the mark of a Lady Gaga or a Beyoncé, is that they don't seem like us: they are idiosyncratic, unique, very little about them is predictable, and they weren't safe bets for the recording executives who gave them a chance.

Lady Gaga and Beyoncé both continue to struggle to escape the limelight of their glamorous personas. After a relatively unsuccessful high-concept third album, Lady Gaga simplified her look, offering us a confessional new album named after her dead aunt, *Joanne*—not to mention recording jazz albums with the grandfatherly Tony Bennett, afflicted with Alzheimer's. Similarly, Beyoncé's album *Lemonade* was a very personal meditation on her troubled marriage with Jay-Z. But when the Academy Awards returned from the pandemic in 2022, Gaga and Beyoncé once again retreated to mascara and gowns.

A t the age of sixteen in 2006, **Bo Burnham** first began posting videos of himself singing and playing guitar in his bedroom. His pun-riddled jokester songs "Bo' Fo' Sho'" and "My Whole Family (Thinks I'm Gay)" went viral on YouTube. By 2022, his comedy albums and specials had been viewed more than five hundred million times, and he earned offers from Hollywood, a special on Comedy Central, a theater tour, and a deal with Netflix. By bypassing the traditional routes to stand-up comedy success, he demonstrated that social media could be a formidable incubator for comedy. Burnham cultivated his social media career into comedy specials, appearances in mainstream movies and directing his own movies (*Eighth Grade*) and dramatic specials on HBO (*Rothaniel*).

Justin Bieber entered a local talent contest in his hometown of Stratford, Ontario, at the age of twelve in 2007. He came in second. His mother, Pattie Mallette, then uploaded YouTube videos of his performances for family and friends who missed the competition. The YouTube videos—Justin singing covers of Usher and Chris Brown—took on a life of their own. The record executive Scooter Braun accidentally clicked on Bieber's videos when searching for videos of a different singer. Impressed, Braun located Bieber's school and finally contacted Mallette. "I wanted to build him up more on YouTube first," he explained. "We supplied more content. I said: 'Justin, sing like there's no one in the room. But let's not use expensive cameras. We'll give it to kids, let them do the work, so that they feel like it's theirs.' "[10]

In a blink, Justin Bieber went from nowhere to the White House. He released his first full-length studio album, *My World 2.0*, in 2010. It debuted at or near number one in several countries, was certified triple platinum in the US, and contained his single "Baby." In just one weekend, he headlined at Madison Square Garden, taped a performance for Dick Clark's New Year's Eve special in Las Vegas, performed in Chicago, and sang for Barack and Michelle Obama at the White House.

In 2022, Bieber announced that that he would be canceling his remaining tour dates that fall in order to prioritize his health after being diagnosed with Ramsay Hunt syndrome, a virus related to chickenpox that can cause facial paralysis. That notwithstanding, Bieber thrives on Instagram with more than 262 million followers—a fact not lost on the marketing community. A social media *influencer* is a so-called content creator who has established credibility in a specific industry, has access to a huge audience, and can persuade others to buy products based on their recommendations. They can be celebrities like **Selena Gomez**, who arrive with a prepackaged fan base, or enterprising users of YouTube, Instagram, and TikTok who build their revenues based on their numbers of views and followers.

Lynette Adkins had been working at Amazon when she realized that she was earning more money from her self-posted YouTube videos and brand sponsorships than in her day job. She quit when she was twenty-three and urged her followers to likewise find fulfillment by abandoning their white-collar jobs. She turned the video camera around and talked about her own experiences. "I'm currently trying to unlearn a lot of things that I grew up learning around work and money," she said. Her postings began with a how-to video for Black women growing out their natural hair and ranged from household budgeting to step-by-step advice for others to strike out on their own. Content creators like Adkins are one of the fastest-growing job categories in the US. She went from virtually nowhere in 2021 to 180,000 paid subscribers on YouTube in late 2022.[11]

Social media hasn't only democratized our culture, as Lebowitz argues; it also threatens to unmoor the American Republic. Today we are living in the unruly democracy of the Founders' nightmares—anyone can become a celebrity with influence from their numbers of fans, like it or not. The American body politic itself has likewise felt topsy-turvy and alienating. Donald Trump used Twitter not only to grow and sustain his celebrity but also to position himself as the one populist in a presidential race. There's a reason why so many political commentators and comedians alike described Donald Trump as someone who had more in common with your crazy bigoted grandfather than he does with any past president. Trump carried out a prime requirement of social media celebrities: he perfectly reflected the values and characteristics of his base.

Where does this leave us when the barriers to acquiring celebrity have virtually disappeared? It means that a thirteen-year-old boy named Ryan McKenna, who was sitting in the crowd at the 2018 Super Bowl, can become instantly famous by snapping a selfie with Justin Timberlake when the singer waded into the crowd. The photo went viral on Instagram, and today the "Selfie Kid" is no longer a cute nickname but McKenna's identity. His Instagram account (@selfiekid) has over 189,000 followers and includes selfies with a range of celebrities from Billie Eilish to Super Bowl MVP Patrick Mahomes. Now celebrities seek out Ryan for the exposure he offers them.

The Super Bowl itself has become a super-spreader event for celebrity and commercialism. Thirty seconds of airtime can cost as much as $7 million. In 2022, Matt Damon pitched Crypto.com on NBC, while the in-stadium crowd competing for free network exposure included Kendall Jenner, Justin Bieber, Kanye West, Ben Affleck and Jennifer Lopez, Dwayne "The Rock" Johnson, Drake, Will Ferrell, Ryan Reynolds, Sean Penn, LeBron James, Mark Wahlberg, and Ellen DeGeneres and Portia de Rossi.

Today, social media has eliminated the marketers in the middle and given everyone a platform. Fame has become ubiquitous. A working definition of celebrities used to be that they were those people for whom there were more people who knew them than they knew in return. But, as TV commentator Chris Hayes argues, it is no longer a novelty that more people know us than we know: "Never before in history have so many people been under the gaze of so many strangers."[12] We can all acquire thousands of followers on Facebook and become celebrities, at least in our minds. And yet these relationships are asymmetrical and deeply unsatisfying.

The recent evolution of the species we may call *celebritus erectus* bears a certain resemblance to the theory of animal reproduction called *r/K* selection (so named for mathematical symbols). The theory, developed by ecologists E. O. Wilson and Robert MacArthur, posits that animal species use one of two basic parenting strategies to reproduce and survive when faced with limited resources. The *K*-strategy parents typically produce only a few offspring who are large, require substantial parental investment of time and energy, and live for a long time. These are the elephants and whales. They are best suited for growth in a stable environment like a savanna or an ocean.

The r-strategy parents, who live in an unstable environment, produce many small offspring, most of whom do not survive, and invest little parental resources in them individually. Think lemmings, cod, and cockroaches. They are designed to overwhelm a volatile environment where sheer numbers will help a lucky few survive.

Celebrities have moved between both strategies over the past century. During the Golden Age of Hollywood, the studios nourished a few carefully chosen stars who were pampered and surrounded by entourages, not unlike pilot fish living off sharks and whales. But when social media and the volatile Age of the Internet arrived, more and more celebrities arrived, each living on their wits and willing to take the risks in an environment where anything goes, anyone can try, and anyone can win— though most won't.

Andy Warhol notoriously once said that in the future everyone will be world famous for fifteen minutes. Or did he? When pressed, he admitted that he actually did not say the aphorism most identified with him. His words just live on in social media.[13]

CHAPTER 6

HOW CELEBRITIES HIJACKED HEROES

When the Czech leader Václav Havel met Paul Newman in 1990, Havel blurted out that the actor was "such a big legend that I didn't believe he physically exists."[1]

Why is this strange? Never mind that Havel was a revered writer and dissident who became the first president of the Czech Republic and a bona fide national hero. Face-to-face with a celebrity, he could not separate his own hard-earned worldly feats from the aura created by a Hollywood movie star.

This slope started to become slippery in the mid-1980s. A defining moment was when celebrities invaded the once-soporific haunts of the mostly male, mostly white Washington press corps. It likely began when a respected young journalist, Michael Kelly of the *Baltimore Sun*, surprised everyone by inviting a sought-after source named Fawn Hall as his guest to the White House Correspondents' Dinner in 1987. Hall had been the document-shredding secretary of Oliver North, a central figure in what became known as the Iran-Contra affair. Her appearance generated a media frenzy—and headlines for the *Baltimore Sun*. The following year, Kelly doubled down by bringing to the same dinner yet another notorious woman, Donna Rice, presidential candidate Gary Hart's campaign-wrecking companion on the yacht *Monkey Business.*

People and other magazines like *Vanity Fair* could see the buzzworthy opportunities and profits ahead in these Washington dinners. So we joined the celebrity sweepstakes by inviting glamorati ranging from Barbra Streisand to Anita Hill. Memorably for me, I once seated Supreme Court justice Sandra Day O'Connor at the same table with NFL fullback John Riggins. As the speeches droned on, the bored Riggins lost patience. "Come on, Sandy, baby, loosen up!" he said repeatedly to the Supreme Court justice, before passing out, dead drunk, on the floor. I turned around just in time to see two of our editors lifting Riggins upright by the armpits and escorting him out of the room. (A few years later, when Riggins appeared as an actor in a local play, O'Connor and her husband dropped off a bouquet of roses with a note saying that his performance was fine but he still needed "to loosen up a bit.")[2]

The White House Correspondents' Dinner all but disappeared for several years when Trump declined to attend during his presidency and when it was not held during the height of the pandemic. But in 2022, what was once called the Nerd Prom roared back with a crowd of 2,600 that included Kim Kardashian and Pete Davidson, Brooke Shields, Caitlyn Jenner, Drew Barrymore, and Martha Stewart—all of them monetizing on celebrification. In the larger picture, though, what was once a sober occasion to honor heroes in our political life, perhaps to poke gentle fun at some of them, became an embarrassing celebrity sideshow, put on by an aristocracy of A-listers.

Not just in America but all around the world there is a thriving international marketplace for celebrities. Demand is high, and so is the supply, thanks to social media. It is a star-making machine that serves up celebrities for consumption—who in turn lend their endorsements to thousands of products.

But as celebrities have proliferated and gone viral, they have crowded our traditional heroes out of the public arena and out of our collective consciousness. The result is that the distinctions between heroism and celebrity are being lost. A 2011 study of the historical change in the different values communicated by TV programs aimed at nine-to-eleven-year-old children found that the "desire for fame" was their number-one value in 2007, rising from number fifteen (out of sixteen) in 1997. The authors attributed this change to the technology-enhanced growth of individualistic values at the expense of community or familial values.[3] Virtually every study since then has shown a similar rise in the value individuals, including children, assign to fame and a decline in the values of community.

People yearn to join the celebrity ecosystem, no matter how they can achieve it. When the man who shot the Beatles' John Lennon, Mark David Chapman, most recently applied for parole, he explained, "I assassinated him . . . because he was very, very, very famous, and that's the only reason, and I was very, very, very much seeking self-glory."[4] In Santa Fe, Texas, in 2018, a seventeen-year-old student opened fire at his high school, killing ten people. He told investigators afterwards that he spared certain students "so he could have his story told."[5]

It is easier to seek glory by killing people than it is to walk the road of heroes. To imagine yourself a hero is to imagine yourself going through trial, risk, self-sacrifice, and, often, injury. It demands courage and conviction to save people. Opportunities to perform real heroics are rare and random; you can't invent them—though some celebrity seekers have been known to try.

Thus, the stumbling block of heroics. Celebrity can be accessed more easily, and celebrities can go through phases, bypass the elites, and adapt to technologies like movies, television, and social media. Heroes can morph into celebrities because of these technologies, but the opposite is difficult. The creation stories for heroes, the ennobling act or acts, remain outside the reach of any scripted superhero falsities or self-aggrandizement on social media.

The frailties of movie stars, rock stars, sports superstars, and royals are central to their appeal. We gain a seeming intimacy that makes us comfortable judging them. When I interviewed President-Elect Bill Clinton and Hillary Rodham Clinton in Little Rock in December 1992, Mrs. Clinton, who at that time had never met Princess Diana, took a freshly published *People* cover story about Diana's troubled marriage from my hands and, looking at it, exclaimed, "Oh, she never should have married so young!"

What Hillary's devilish comment shows us is that gossip is a cross-cultural lingua franca. That is a comment she could have made just about anywhere in the world and people would have known whom she was talking about. She was well aware that celebrity gossip is the world's backyard fence. It is particularly ironic that this was said by Hillary Clinton, herself the object of many judgments over the backyard fence.

Gossiping about celebrities may seem to be a light diversion to those of us looking for cheap entertainment. We certainly thought so at *People* when we gave the prime real estate of the back page to a compilation of celebrities' quotes called "Chatter." But today the professional community takes a more severe approach. As the radio and television host Dr. Drew Pinsky writes, in *The Mirror Effect*, "When people join together to gossip about an individual or group, they are collaborating in an effort to make themselves feel better about their own lives. However, they are also expressing a deep-seated aggression—a response that's triggered by narcissistic envy."[6]

Gossip clearly has multiple functions in human societies. One of them is that it provides vicarious entertainment. As the columnist Liz Smith put it in 1978, "Gossip is news running ahead of itself in a red satin dress."[7] Gossip is a language understood within communities as a form of grooming and social bonding; it is how we explore our place in the world—what is acceptable and what is not acceptable. It is often considered socially taboo and dismissed as scurrilous defamation.

But in 2021, two Dartmouth professors, Luke Chang and Eshin Jolly, co-authored a study to determine why people gossip and what function it serves. Gossip is not necessarily spreading rumors or saying bad things about other people, but it can include small talk in-person or online, such as having a private chat during a Zoom meeting, explained the researchers. Prior research had found that approximately 14 percent of people's daily conversations are gossip and primarily neutral in tone. What Chang and Jolly found and published in *Current Biology* was that gossip enables social connections and enables learning from others when direct observation is not possible. As Jolly says, "Gossip can be useful because it helps people learn through the experience of others, while enabling them to become closer to each other in the process."[8]

Alice Marwick and danah boyd similarly observe that gossip can be thought of as a type of "social grooming" similar to that practiced in the forest by apes who fastidiously groom each other's fur.[9]

The gossip boom during the current tell-all era has been harder on our heroes than on our celebrities. We have less tolerance for flaws in our heroes. It is as if we measure them by entertainment values. The story lines we assign to them want excitement and triumph but do not allow for the inconsistencies and flaws the Greeks knew we all have. We struggle to reconcile the shining image of Nelson Mandela with his imperious manner, quick temper, multiple marriages, and often discomforting political alliances. Today's cancel culture would have been troubled by his justifications of political violence, not to mention his affinity for business elites.

The result? We end up with a scarcity of universally accepted public heroes amid an overabundance of flawed celebrities. The internet and the constantly churning news cycle have eliminated the need for intermediaries to determine who will be made famous. There is a thriving international marketplace of proliferating celebrities ready to step into the breach.

You can see the result of this trend on the landing page of *People*'s online archive of its covers. The category titled "Real People" is dominated by crime victims and reality show stars. Finding more stirringly heroic real people, such as Chesley "Sully" Sullenberger, the US Airways pilot who safely crash-landed his airliner in the Hudson River, requires searching the database. (Sullenberger was later officially anointed an American hero by being played by Tom Hanks in the movie version of the crash story.)

When three everyday heroes emerged in the same week in 2018, it felt like a transit of Venus, a rarity of nature. They were a female pilot who crash-landed her plane safely, a Black customer who wrestled a rifle from a Waffle House shooter in Tennessee, and a Latino policeman in Toronto who risked his life to stop a murderer in a van.

The local media covered all three—the first step in the march toward fame—but then the stories died out before the celebrity-making machinery kicked in. Today that would have required the heroes to skillfully navigate social media. As Alice Marwick and danah boyd put it in their study of the uses of Twitter by famous people, "Twitter creates a new expectation of intimacy. Rather than handing off fan management to an agent or fan club, celebrity practitioners must expend emotional labor maintaining a network of affective ties with their followers. Thus, even the famous must learn the techniques used by 'regular people' to gain status and attention online. Twitter demonstrates the transformation of 'celebrity' from a personal quality linked to fame to a set of practices that circulate through modern social media."[10]

The Pew Research Center surveyed millennials in 2007 and asked them whom they most admire. A heartening number of them mentioned the names of people who were close to them.

Yet they were almost twice as likely to cite entertainers as they were to mention political figures. And compared with older cohorts, they were more likely to mention entertainers and much less likely to list political figures among their heroes.

Perhaps that's because today's definition of *heroes* is drawn so narrowly. To find them, we tend to default to the military, or superheroes, or to charismatic figures in history. There was a time when we didn't have to choose, when our celebrities and our heroes tended to be one and the same. People became famous for great deeds. Think of Frederick Douglass, Thomas Edison, Amelia Earhart, Muhammad Ali. There are only a precious few left now, like Michelle Obama, Maria Ressa, Greta Thunberg. If we saw their flaws, we accepted their flaws.

Classical mythology has an Age of Heroes—the famous figures who are celebrated in the *Iliad* and the *Odyssey.* The Greeks and especially the Romans situated this age in an irrecoverable past. The Protestant tradition rather similarly situates sainthood in the past—there aren't any modern saints that the Protestants recognize.

Meanwhile, we seem to have forgotten the idea that heroes—especially tragic heroes—*are* flawed. If we compare the idea of the hero in history with the emerging celebrity, some polarities are clear.

> The hero is distinguished by achievement; the celebrity is distinguished by image or trademark.
> The hero creates fame by extraordinary actions and achievements; the celebrity is created by the media.
> The hero is a big person; the celebrity is a big name.
> The hero represents community values; the celebrity stands for individual values.
> The hero is sacrificing; the celebrity is selfish.
> The passage of time enlarges the hero; the passage of time diminishes the celebrity.

Sometimes the worlds of the celebrity and the hero can align in common cause. During World War II, the American government enlisted celebrities like movie stars Donna Reed and Marlene Dietrich to sell bonds, boost morale among soldiers, and perform other political functions—a phenomenon that continues to the present day. Interviewed by CBS News in 2017, Mary Owen, the daughter of Donna Reed, likened the pin-up girls, whose images filled the barracks of American soldiers during World War II, to talismans—suggesting that for the soldiers, those pin-ups functioned in an almost religious way, carrying unseen psychic and even spiritual energy in the archetypal projections we make onto celebrities and thereby giving the men inspiration and hope.[11] In the same story, there was a telling exchange between the late actress Marsha Hunt, who worked Saturday nights at the Hollywood Canteen during World War II, and Martha Teichner, a CBS reporter:

INTERVIEWER: "Was it flattering to you, or uncomfortable, to be touched by so many people?"

MARSHA HUNT: "It was fame; they were dancing with fame, not with Marsha Hunt. It was a privilege to be among them, and to give them a lift of morale, which it certainly did. I guess there might have been some pride in it, because you weren't sure that any of them would ever come home. So you did that little thing, you signed your silly name, and it seemed to matter to them and to their folks back home."[12]

Corporations, like governments, have struggled to use images of celebrity to serve their purposes. When Norwegian Air's first Boeing 737s took to the skies in 2002, the airline wanted to make a statement about how they were pushing boundaries against their competition. So they adorned the tails of their aircraft with portraits of personalities from all the Nordic countries. Today, they have tail-fin heroes from Spain, France, England, Ireland, and Scotland.

In most cases, the acts of heroism for which the tail-fin heroes are known seem to be distinctly nineteenth-century phenomena: there are almost as many heroes generated before the nineteenth century as there are contemporary heroes. When you try to compare the categories, you quickly see that Norwegian largely picked their heroes from a settled history.

Over the years, Americans of every passion and vocation have attempted to define their heroes through their own halls of fame. There is the Baseball Hall of Fame and a Rock & Roll Hall of Fame—and also an Off-Road Motorsports Hall of Fame, a Rockabilly Hall of Fame, an Internet Hall of Fame, and a Bowling Hall of Fame. But first was the once renowned but now forgotten relic known as the Hall of Fame for Great Americans, formally dedicated in New York City on Memorial Day, May 30, 1901.[13]

Conceived by the chancellor of New York University, Dr. Henry Mitchell MacCracken, and financed by Helen Miller Gould, the daughter of financier Jay Gould, the first hall of fame in the US was built as a marble colonnade on top of a bluff in the Bronx and outfitted with bronze tablets designed by Tiffany honoring each recipient. In 1901, George Washington was elected unanimously by all ninety-seven electors. Abraham Lincoln, Benjamin Franklin, Thomas Jefferson, and John Adams were likewise elected. The others included Daniel Webster, Ulysses S. Grant, John Marshall, Robert Fulton, Jonathan Edwards, Samuel F. B. Morse, and David Farragut.

The list grew to 102 names and included only two women (Clara Barton and Susan B. Anthony) and only two African Americans (Booker T. Washington and George Washington Carver). Writers and performers like Louisa May Alcott and P. T. Barnum were, if anything, conspicuously absent by today's standards. Celebrities were then curiosities, but most of the heroes of the past century were the stars in a universe of white men. Today, the Hall of Fame for Great Americans in the Bronx is only a relic. The busts in the hall, sculpted by Daniel Chester French and other noted artists, gather more dust than praise.

Heroes are now so much an endangered species that they have acquired their own benefactors. The Carnegie Hero Fund Commission has given out more than ten thousand medals honoring individual acts of bravery since 1904. The nonprofit Heroic Imagination Project has identified thirty-four qualities special to heroes, including behavior that is voluntary and intentional, done in service of people or communities in need, involves some degree of personal cost or risk, and is done without need for recompense or gain.

To be fair, many celebrities have found ways to identify themselves with worthy causes. As the joke goes, a movie star without a cause is like a woodpecker without a tree. After the TV star Gilda Radner died at age forty-two, her husband, Gene Wilder, co-founded Gilda's Club, a chain of cancer support facilities. When *People* brought Princess Diana to Chicago in 1996, she hosted a luncheon there for Gilda's Club that was their biggest fundraiser ever. An event for the Pediatric AIDS Foundation in LA drew Tom Hanks, Steven Spielberg, Christie Brinkley, and Sandy Koufax. All the assembled celebrity power in these cases benefitted everyone (especially *People*).

Jane Fonda paved the way for many movie stars to embrace political activism—often, though, they were white. However, when Louisville healthcare worker Breonna Taylor was killed by police in her apartment in 2020, stars like John Legend, Selena Gomez, Kayne West, and Cardi B took up her cause. Others who marched and raised money for Taylor's family included Ariana Grande, Beyoncé, The Weeknd, and Billie Eilish.

Hero worship can start early. So can celebrity worship. For any kid who grew up in St. Louis in the 1950s, there was only one celebrity in town: the great baseball player Stan Musial. Musial was our Galahad, our Achilles, our Hector—a modest, decent soft-spoken man who did more than anyone to raise St. Louis to its reputation as a good sports town where the fans even clap for the opposing team's players. He was our antidote to the malaise left by the Greenlease kidnapping and murder.

The inevitable moment of reckoning came for me a couple of years ago at a St. Louis Cardinals' spring training game in Florida. A friend ushered me into the owners' box, and there stood Stan, in his red blazer and loopy grin, talking with his friend and another Cardinals great, Red Schoendienst.

I had one chance to ask him a question, and I blew it. I asked about the moment in the 1946 World Series against the Boston Red Sox when outfielder Enos Slaughter scored on a madcap run for home plate that gave the series to the Cardinals. Musial laughed and answered a question he had heard too many times. "Slaughter just outran the ball," he said in his oddly wheezy, high-pitched voice. "He just beat the ball to the plate."

What I did not ask him was what he thought about playing at Sportsman's Park, the brooding, gothic pile of steel on St. Louis's North Side, where the city's two professional baseball teams, the Cardinals and the Browns, played. As you walked toward it on a dark night, the ballpark loomed like a cathedral, a study in hooded arches. At first you glimpsed only flashes of green sliced by rusting steel columns. It took a minute for your eyes to adjust to this—baseball was still in black and white on television, and here was a new world of blinding white and green. The chalky basepaths and the balls themselves seemed to be an unworldly, incandescent white.

When Musial played, the crowd was white too, with one exception. As he stood coiled in the batter's box, behind him a phalanx of Black faces looked back at him from the right-field pavilion. In those days, Black people were limited first by law and then by custom to sitting only in the right-field stands. I remember wondering at the time what they thought of this arrangement.

But I hesitated to ask Musial about the ballpark or the integration of baseball teams he had witnessed when Jackie Robinson arrived. Celebrities do not typically help us to better understand ourselves and our world. They are more likely to reinforce our preconceptions than to lead us to new ideas. Consequently, the culture feels recycled, mired in the same nostalgia I felt when I met Musial. We'll need to look elsewhere for people who help us bridge the gap between who we are and who we want to be.

CHAPTER 7

CELEBRITY WORSHIP

W here are we now?

Well, Dorothy, we're not in Kansas anymore.

In the first twenty years of this century, celebrity culture erupted full-throated from the sidelines to become a dominant influence in our lives and in our societies. It has changed the character of youth and adolescence worldwide and contributed to the political and class divisions that have besieged modern democracies. It has promoted individualism at the cost of the social capital that societies need. Today we are no longer sitting around our campfires. We are gazing into phones and mirrors.

As Robert Putnam documented in *Bowling Alone*, civic engagement and trust have declined in America since the arrival of the baby boomers and television sets in the late 1950s. Americans' attendance at club meetings in 2005 was a third of what it had been in 1975; Americans entertained friends and family sixteen times a year in 1980 but only eight times in 2005.[1] Putnam's works discuss the weakening of community and the loneliness and alienation of individuals in American society in the earliest days of the twenty-first century.

Putnam assigned most of the blame to the isolating effects of electronic entertainment—now made only more omnipresent by the arrival of smartphones and social media in the early 2000s. Not only do they reach into all of our lives; the content they deliver also has promoted a global addiction to fame and celebrity that has divided us even further, starting in childhood.

How did this happen? What do we really know about the rise of celebrity in our culture today—the quest for it, its command of public attention, and the damage it is doing to fans and celebrities alike? Is celebrity worship caused by the long decline in our shared social capital, as documented by Putnam? Have we replaced going to bowling leagues with staying home and bolstering our loneliness by watching celebrities on Instagram?

But it's not so simple. Social scientists will be the first to tell us that correlation is not causation. The link between celebrity worship and social capital could also work the other way around. That is, celebrity worship could well be the machine that powers the breakdown in our communities. Celebrities and their brands draw us into the internet and social media and away from the world of real companionship. We wind up looking at them and not each other.

Finally, there is the third possibility that celebrity worship and low social capital are both the results of an independent factor that affects both—the rise of electronic media, especially since the arrival of the internet 2.0.

Since the year 2000, a slew of academic and journalistic studies have taken on these questions and produced conclusions that are both convincing and disturbing.

The first is that the desire of individuals to acquire fame and celebrity is carried by generations, especially among children and preadolescents. In Britain in 2006, the organizers of National Children's Day asked children under ten years old to reveal their Christmas wish list. The desire to be famous or "being a celebrity" emerged at the top of the list, followed by "good looks" and "being rich."[2]

The desire for fame is one of the best examples of this mismatch between what we want and what actually nourishes us.

From our youngest ages, people crave it. According to one study, fame is the biggest goal in life for children in the US ages ten to twelve.[3] In a 2017 survey of one thousand British children, the most popular choice for a future career was "YouTuber."[4]

According to a survey done by the *Washington Post* and Harvard University in 2005, 31 percent of American teenagers thought they would become famous one day.[5] Statistically, this is just not possible. Adults are less willing to freely admit that they want to be famous, but according to Gallup, 92 percent of American adults say that *other* people believe "a person is successful if they are rich, have a high-profile career, or are well-known."[6]

The ugly truth is, despite how much we desire it, fame is terrible for happiness. A 2012 study in the journal *Psychology and Marketing* found that intense personal worship of celebrities most affects female adolescents who acquire "a poor body image."[7] Other studies have demonstrated that materialism and compulsive buying were significantly correlated with "celebrity worship" as was lower self-concept clarity.

One effect of the rapidly increasing number of reality television shows such as *Survivor* and *The Celebrity Apprentice* is that it now seems much easier to be famous. Reality TV gives people fame for being themselves, no special skills or achievement necessary.

At the same time, entertainment is increasingly seen as being central to the global internet-based society. In his book *Fame Junkies*, Jake Halpern cites a study of 653 middle school students near Rochester, New York, who seem representative of the United States as a whole demographically in terms of future ideal job occupations. The result of the survey was that a remarkable 43.4 percent chose to become "the personal assistant to a very famous singer or movie star."[8] Simple proximity to a celebrity seemed to be an ideal occupational choice for these middle school students in the United States.

For those with a desire for fame, the quick rise to celebrity through participation in reality TV shows is particularly appealing for young males. This may reflect a need for social attention and acceptance, which is the promise of many marketing campaigns. Surveys of teenagers show, in terms of their wish list, that American teenagers in the twenty-first century overwhelming chose to gain "fame" over all other attributes, including intelligence or wealth.[9]

One of the first television programs that depicted the value and advantages of being famous was the Robin Leach television show *Lifestyles of the Rich and Famous*. Such programs help people draw the conclusion that becoming famous makes life better.[10]

This focus on fame and celebrity can be seen as a type of addiction. Lynn E. McCutcheon and her associates have attempted to classify degrees of celebrity absorption according to what they call the Celebrity Worship Scale (CWS). They identified three ascending stages of the malady:

Low worship involves light interests such as watching and reading about a celebrity.

Mid-level, when celebrity worship takes on a social character with personal feelings of affection and familiarity.

High worship, when celebrity worship includes a mixture of empathy with a celebrity's successes and failures, over-identification with the celebrity, compulsive behaviors, and obsessive interest in the details of a celebrity's life, including delusions of having actual relationships with a celebrity. People who lack meaningful relationships or a strong sense of personal identity may become overly absorbed in their attachment to celebrities.[11]

In 2021, the Pew Research Center found that roughly one-quarter of all US adults now use Twitter. Moreover, a minority of extremely active tweeters produced the overwhelming majority of all tweets made by US adults. During the period of June 12 through September 12 of 2021, the top 25 percent of Twitter users, measured by tweet volume, produced 97 percent of all tweets (which includes original tweets as well as retweets, replies, and quote tweets). This group produced a median of sixty-five tweets per month on average. Moreover, 34 percent of Twitter users say that the site has increased how much they know about the lives of celebrities and public figures.[12]

If asked whether Twitter is good or bad for democracy, a narrow margin of US adults say it is bad for democracy (38 percent versus 37 percent). But Republican Twitter users (including Republican-leaning independents) are roughly twice as likely as Democrats and Democratic leaners to say the site is bad for American democracy (60 percent versus 28 percent). Conversely, roughly half of Democrats who use the site say it is good for American democracy—just 17 percent of Republican users say the same.

This disparity suggests that celebrities can reach out to their fans easily on Twitter—especially those who are Republicans or lean Republican. And that brings us back to the worlds of Jenny Lind, P. T. Barnum, Sarah Bernhardt, and Annie Oakley, all of whom rode the energy generated by media innovations like cartes de visite to acquire their own definable celebrity status.

I vividly saw the ugly side of celebrity worship one year at the White House Correspondents' Dinner. My celebrity guests were Dean Cain, then TV's Superman, and Gillian Anderson, who played FBI Special Agent Dana Scully on *The X-Files*. As I led them through the lobby of the Washington Hilton Hotel, a crowd of boisterous young fans who had been restrained behind velvet ropes suddenly surged free. In a scene straight out of Nathanael West's *The Day of the Locust*, they surrounded and besieged the two actors, forcing them to scramble into the chairs atop a shoeshine stand, where they perched and waited until the fans dispersed.

The more pathological precincts of the celebrosphere are defined more brutally. A year after Mark David Chapman killed John Lennon in 1980, John Hinckley Jr. shot Ronald Reagan, at the same Washington Hilton where Cain and Anderson were besieged. His act was an attempt to find fame that would impress the actress Jodie Foster. The actress Rebecca Schaeffer (*My Sister Sam*) was shot and killed in her doorway in 1989 by Robert John Brando, who had been stalking her for three years. She was twenty-one. Andrew Cunanan murdered five people, including Gianni Versace, in 1990. Among just a few of the others who have been stalked by fame seekers and obsessive fans are Nicole Kidman, Elle Macpherson, Ashley Judd, Madonna, Steven Spielberg, and Michael J. Fox.

Researcher Yalda Uhls has written personally about the origins of the pursuit of fame. As she writes, "In the new millennium, people face messages highlighting the significance of fame everywhere they look. Not only in reality television shows such as *Keeping Up with the Kardashians* and *American Idol*, but also in popular fictional TV shows, even those targeted to children. After watching some of these shows with my then 9-year-old daughter, I grumbled about the drastic change in 'values,'" she continues. "Worried that I was becoming one of those predictable adults who lament that things were much better in the past, I decided to test my hypothesis."[13]

Professor Uhls conducted a study with Dr. Patricia Greenfield at UCLA that sought to rank the values communicated by TV shows watched by tween audiences (age nine to eleven) over the past forty years. The value of fame rose from the bottom of the value rankings in 1967 (number fifteen out of sixteen) to become the number-one value communicated to preteens on popular television in 2007. In contrast, community feeling (to be part of a group) fell sharply, from number one to number eleven in recent decades. "We wondered if the synergy between the fame-oriented content of popular TV shows and the opportunity to post online videos and status updates for 'friends' and strangers created the perfect storm for a desire for fame," the researchers said. "In our discussions, we asked preteens what they wanted in their future. Their number one choice? Fame."[14]

Uhls points out that in the twenty-first century, TV content socializes children more than at any other point in its history. Even though children today have a myriad of media choices, they still watch televised content an average of an hour a day, on the traditional sets, or online, on smartphones, or iPads. If the stories kids see on TV are about young people achieving great success and renown, acting individually, it's only natural for kids to start wanting this for themselves.

The common themes of this research revealed a desire for fame and the perceived benefits of social status, power and influence, improved lifestyle, celebrity emulation, and increased happiness. The following six items captured the motivation and perceived benefits of fame expressed by the participants in the study:

1. One day I would like to be famous.
2. I love the idea of becoming a famous person.
3. I would like to be famous because it would give me a higher social status.
4. I would like to be famous because other people would perceive me as having more power and influence.
5. The lifestyle of famous celebrities appeals to me a lot.
6. If I were famous I would be happier.

Note the ubiquitous first-person singular. The hunger for fame is not about "we." In other words, fame—which rewards individuals—has grown in influence, while those values promoting communities, family, and tradition have diminished.

Thanks to technology, fame and individualism are promoted in places other than on TV shows. The nine-to-eleven-year-old tweens are busily soaking up the same emphasis on fame from the internet and on social media. In addition, the researchers argued, as learning environments move toward high technology, as living environments become increasingly urbanized, as education levels increase, and as people become wealthier, psychological development moves in the direction of increasing individualism, while traditional, family, and community values decline.[15]

The results can be measured. A sweeping analysis of eighty-five samples of American university students over a period from 1979 to 2006 revealed that narcissistic personality traits increased 30 percent.[16] In the same period, US students gained a greater desire for money, and empathy levels dropped over 40 percent, with the biggest drop after the year 2000. The valuing of tradition has also decreased across the generations. These differences can be transmitted to tweens in the informal learning environments of popular TV programs aimed at them and are omnipresent on the internet.[17]

Communitarian values—defined as community feeling, tradition, and benevolence—also declined in relative importance from the mid-sixties to the twenty-first century. Community feeling started out as the top-ranked value in 1967 and fell to number eleven. Tradition was ranked fourth in 1967 and fell to fifteenth place in 2007. Benevolence went from second place to twelfth place across the decades. Of all the values assessed, those three showed the largest declines in relative importance.

Given that the chimera of celebrity permeates popular television, and that a lifestyle of enormous success, wealth, and renown is depicted as normal for adolescent characters, tweens are likely to believe that this lifestyle is entirely possible and easy to achieve. Alas, most of the teenagers and young adults who want fame and celebrity will sooner or later be disappointed.

Perhaps as a result, we seem eager to seize on the flaws of the rich and famous and reduce them somehow to our level. It's a kind of social-leveling schadenfreude, a reassuring message that moderates our envy. Every day social media pours into the world a river of unfiltered gossip—"I just heard . . ."—that usually predicts ten of the last two celebrity divorces. The snarkiest tone afflicts not "real celebrities" (that's an oxymoron like "athleisure" you might have hoped would never be necessary) but rather the famous-for-being-famous reality show para-celebrities such as Cardi B, Elisabeth Hasselbeck, and Britney Spears's ex-husband Kevin Federline (who inevitably went from K-Fed to Fed-Ex).

In their most recent shape-shifting, as presented in magazines like the one I edited, the portrayals of celebrities' lives have too often become what Joyce Carol Oates calls *pathographies*—studies in alcoholism, divorce, sexual abuse, and racism.[18] At *People*, I used to think we could rely on three types of cover stories: Di, Diet, and Dying. Bizarrely, all three came together when the princess was driven to death by the public gaze of paparazzi in Paris. She was young, beautiful, and dead—our society's answer to Madame Bovary and Marilyn Monroe.

In this 24/7 celebrity news cycle (another bizarre new phrase), there is not time for any kind of compelling narrative to build up. Public fascination is ripped out of the ground before it flowers.

In the Golden Age of Hollywood, the narrative arc of a star's career could be neatly compressed as seen through the eyes of a studio boss. For some reason, this tale originally centered on the TV actor Hugh O'Brian, but today we might think of a fresher star, and the life cycle runs something like this:

FIRST STAGE:	Who's Andrew Garfield?
SECOND STAGE:	Get me Andrew Garfield.
THIRD STAGE:	Get me an Andrew Garfield type.
FOURTH STAGE:	Get me a young Andrew Garfield.
FIFTH AND FINAL STAGE:	Who's Andrew Garfield?[19]

In the hands of some celebrities, fame can be a tool to help them do better in the world. Others, though, are plunged into a reality-distortion field. When my friend Jim Gaines was the editor of *LIFE*, he was planning a cover story on the actor Mel Gibson for its December issue. Arrangements were made with the publicists, an interviewer, a photographer—all of them approved.

LIFE then did some market research, which suggested that a religious topic might outsell Mel Gibson on the December cover. So the editors switched the cover subject, and artwork, to a new topic: specifically, God.

Jim told me he had to call Mel's publicist and inform him that their client would no longer be on the cover.

"Who is going to be on the cover?" asked the publicist.

Jim paused and said, "God."

Longer pause. Then the publicist said, "Mel is going to be very disappointed."

The good news is that Mel and God are still on speaking terms.

CHAPTER 8

THE SELLING OF CELEBRITY

Celebrities can go places where heroes are not allowed. Mainly, they can sell things. Gwyneth Paltrow can make the case that Goop products agree with her lifestyle, and who can object? So can Harry Styles with his gender-neutral nail polish branded as Pleasing. And Mariah Carey with McDonald's and her Black Irish liquor line. Nicole Richie with sleepwear. Rita Ora with duvets. Jennifer Garner with Capital One and Neutrogena.

Since the turn of the century, these and many other celebrities have created personal brands with spin-offs that keep their products in the spotlight. So Iman creates a cosmetics line for people of color. Backstreet Boy AJ McLean has a nail-polish brand named after his daughters. Ariana Grande, Billie Eilish, Chiara Ferragni, and Addison Rae all have makeup and skin-care lines. Sarah Jessica Parker has shoes. The Olsen twins have beauty products and fashion lines. Cardi B is at *Playboy* as its "creative director in residence." Celebrities are selling us all they can, all the time. As Susan Douglas, a media professor at the University of Michigan, puts it, "There's a battle for visibility. What is the scarcest resource? People's attention. You have to keep your name out there or people will forget about you."[1]

The name recognition that celebrities provide is used to personify corporations and establish brand identities for otherwise faceless products. When it works, the product itself becomes a celebrity. Celebrity branding imbues companies with personalities—and with risks. The man named Ye (yes, the celebrity-obsessed Kanye West) sold sneakers for Adidas before he blew up the deal with his defiant and offensive antisemitic remarks in late 2022.[2]

The basketball player Michael Jordan endorses not only the expected Nike, Gatorade, and Wheaties but also bowling alleys, Chevy, and men's fashions. The actor Michael B. Jordan was in one of the highest-grossing superhero films of all time, *Black Panther*, but he decided to partner with tea brand Brisk to direct a sixty-second spot called "Hidden Hustle." The objective was to illustrate how the tea brand wants to enable and support young creators who do things differently—and to sell both tea and tickets.

As Jordan explains, "When choosing what brand to work with, you have to choose one that coincides with your goals. You are defined by what you say no to. I'm not the type of guy to chase money or projects. It has to mean something and fit into the blueprint of what you want."[3]

Accordingly, celebrities can be present at the creation. In 2021, Dolly Parton launched a lifestyle brand aimed at developing products in fashion, jewelry, and housewares. As her partners at the brand-licensing firm IMG put it, "Together, we look forward to building cohesive lifestyle brand products that will celebrate Dolly and bring her iconic style and personality to her millions of fans worldwide in engaging new ways."[4] Dolly was so sensitive to staying on-brand as a country singer that in 2022 she refused her nomination to the Rock & Roll Hall of Fame. (The Rock Hall rejected her request to pull out.)

The stakes have become increasingly large. Kim Kardashian's shapewear brand, SKIMS, launched in 2019 and by early 2022 was valued at $1.6 billion.[5] Her sister Kylie sold a majority stake in their cosmetics line for $1.2 billion. According to *Forbes*, between his salary and endorsement deals, Kobe Bryant had earned $600 million by the time he died in 2020.[6]

Thus singer/songwriter/TV personality Ray J has transformed himself from Kim Kardashian's sex-tape partner into a tech entrepreneur. He launched Raycon, the stylish new celeb-powered collection that includes items like rose gold wireless headphones, digital smartwatches, and portable cannon-style speakers.

The first issue of *People* featured on its cover a celebrity who was very much a stand-in for a product—Mia Farrow, dressed and made-up for her role as Daisy Buchanan in the 1974 film version of *The Great Gatsby*. She was selling the movie, and *People* was selling its first issue. She was finally allowed to return to her real self, her hair tousled and making eye contact with the reader, for the cover of *People*'s twentieth-anniversary issue.

Heroes almost never try to endorse products—it is somehow a violation of the trust we have given them. But technology does not differentiate between heroes and celebrities. All that matters is whether the message is on-brand or off-brand. As one marketer summed it up for the *New York Times* recently, "Brand is everything, and everything is brand."[7]

Not surprisingly, some celebrities have literally insured their body parts—and publicized it—if only to protect their brands. They include David Beckham (legs), Mariah Carey (voice and legs), Daniel Craig (entire body), Jamie Lee Curtis (legs), America Ferrera (smile), Heidi Klum (legs), Keith Richards (hands), Rihanna (legs), Julia Roberts (smile), and Bruce Springsteen (voice).[8]

Our hope then lies with whose people who have insulated themselves from celebrity and let celebrity come to them. These are often women, and particularly women of color. In just a month after she famously read "The Hill We Climb" at Joe Biden's inauguration, the striking young poet Amanda Gorman turned down $17 million in promotional offers before signing up with Estée Lauder.[9] As of this writing, she has 3.9 million Instagram followers.

In the space of less than a year, the biracial pop singer Olivia Rodrigo won three Grammys, was involved in a White House effort to promote COVID-19 vaccinations among young people in the US, was *Time*'s 2021 Entertainer of the Year, and signed a long-term partnership to be the first-ever brand partner with the billion-dollar beauty startup Glossier Inc. When the night arrived for the Met Gala in New York, Rodrigo posed in a Versace dress that caused a paparazzi scrum.

The dilemma celebrities face is that their brands can become a prison constricting their lives and pursuits, since they're typically not permitted to behave in ways contradicting expectations of their public image. That's why many celebrities create an alter ego, a shadow celebrity self for public consumption, at a safe remove from their real self. The middle-class Samuel Clemens of Hannibal, Missouri, created the iconoclastic writer Mark Twain. Robert Zimmerman of Hibbing, Minnesota, did something of the same when he invented the protest singer Bob Dylan. And Belcalis Almánzar from the South Bronx in New York became the no-filter rapper and influencer Cardi B.

Today, we are trying to look beyond the current technologies and figure out where they are taking us. One such area is social media. Consider the new generation of brand influencers it has suddenly fostered. The scale is astonishing. Kim Kardashian alone has 326 million followers on Instagram, as of September 2022.

What is less well-known is the impact on the millions of followers who participate. Many of them have what researchers call *problematic engagement* with social media influencers "that is common among followers, but not well known or understood." A 2022 study by three Australian scholars estimated the size of the influencer market at $13.8 billion in the US alone.[10] They then looked at what is termed "the dark side of social media influencing." They specifically drew on psychological attachment theory to examine the ways that followers can become attached to and obsessed with influencers.

As they explained, the researchers studied five hundred Instagram users to explore the factors and mechanisms that lead to problematic engagement. Based on attachment theory, they studied two types of attachments: *parasocial relationship* and *sense of belonging*, both of which are key in social media influencing. A parasocial relationship refers to followers' perception of their one-sided relationship with an influencer, and a sense of belonging describes the feeling of being an integral member of the influencer's community. The study results showed that when followers develop attachments both to influencers (a parasocial relationship) and their community (a sense of belonging), it can lead to problematic engagement.

The researchers argued that social media users who are attracted to influencers can become easily attached and engage excessively. Risks include negative consequences such as followers' anxiety and depression, eating disorders, and spending well beyond one's means. If our children are comparing themselves to the fantasy lives they see exhibited by the influencers on social media, it is not surprising that they look into the mirror and find themselves feeling alone together.

Not everything can be pushed through the painful eye of the needle of entertainment values. The ground is moving beneath our feet. The beauty brand BH Cosmetics went bankrupt in 2022, despite signing celebrity influencers Doja Cat and Iggy Azalea. The celebrity brands that seem most entrenched are Rihanna's Fenty Beauty, with a half-billion dollars in revenue; Kylie Jenner's Kylie Cosmetics ("now clean, vegan, cruelty free, gluten free, and paraben free"); and Gwyneth Paltrow's Goop (wellness advice, events, skin care, supplements, and bath salts, among other offerings).

More and more often, the arrival of enormous amounts of money has meant that the lines between public and private, ordinary and famous, proper and improper are narrowing and disappearing. When Paltrow wanted to campaign in 2022 in favor of *Roe v. Wade*, she produced a scented candle called Hands Off My Vagina with proceeds supporting the ACLU. Like women before her ranging from Sarah Bernhardt to Calamity Jane, she knew that defiant celebrity gets attention.

In this sense, the contemporary celebrity text is a story that captures the issues, values, and themes that are working at the heart of American culture. It is one in which the individuals pick up on Dan McAdams's script for highly generative adults:

- ★ I have a special gift.
- ★ I see and am moved by suffering in the world. [Hello, Sting, Brad Pitt, and Angelina Jolie].
- ★ I believe my destiny is to have a positive impact on others.
- ★ I will never abandon these core beliefs.
- ★ I struggle to reconcile my individual strengths and ambitions with my need for love and community.
- ★ Bad things happen to me, but good outcomes follow. My suffering is then redeemed.
- ★ I expect things I have generated will grow and flourish.[11]

The only thing that makes this scenario different for celebrities is that it happens under intense observation by the media and marketers.

Which brings me, at last, to politicians who are celebrities. And vice versa.

The received wisdom is that Donald Trump was an aberration in American political life. Attention to his rise usually focuses on his assiduously cultivated celebrity status and picturesque obsession with acquiring more fame, more praise, and more money.

Yet he was hardly the first celebrated American to make a calculated leap into politics. The military hero Andrew Jackson did so in the Early Republic, becoming the first political celebrity to take advantage of the rise of a new form of media: daily newspapers. As his biographers David and Jeanne Heidler put it, "The use of newspapers in the campaign of 1828 was the most revolutionary aspect of a revolutionary year in American politics . . . the first instance of deliberate image building and mythmaking and of skillful manipulation of public perception and popular opinion."[12]

More recent examples of celebrities who used their name recognition to their advantage politically include California governors Ronald Reagan and Arnold Schwarzenegger, TV stars Al Franken and Fred Thompson (senators from Minnesota and Tennessee, respectively), Clint Eastwood and Sonny Bono (mayors of Carmel and Palm Springs, California, respectively), and the 2003 *American Idol* runner-up Clay Aiken, who in 2022 was defeated for the Democratic nomination in North Carolina's Sixth Congressional District.

Before the arrival of *The Apprentice* in 2004, Donald Trump was a B-list inhabitant of gossip columns who specialized in filing serial bankruptcies and prowling beauty contests. But even then he exhibited a degree of celebrity self-absorption high on the Celebrity Worship Scale. In an eerily prescient column Nora Ephron wrote for *Esquire* in June 1989, she said:

> Here is what interests me about Donald Trump: He wants to be famous. He wants people to talk about him. He wants people to notice him. He wants people to write about him. He wants people to ask him for autographs and recognize him and invade his privacy; not that he seems to have any privacy; he doesn't even seem to have a single solitary thought he manages to keep to himself, so perhaps there's no privacy to invade. Perhaps that's the secret. Who knows? It doesn't matter. I tip my hat to Donald Trump, because except for an occasional churlish moment he seems to be genuinely enjoying the experience of fame in a way that no one in his right

mind ever does, and the fact that he therefore seems not to have any sense or intelligence or taste whatsoever is beside the point. *The man has adapted.*

It speaks to those times that, when Ephron wrote her column, anyone's obsession with fame seemed to be a novelty. During that time, Trump appeared on *People*'s cover regularly, including once in 1990, grinning and grasping $1 million in cash in his arms. I shudder to remember that I was the editor. But frankly, in those days, we thought he was simply a buffoon—a defiant buffoon, to be sure. Once again, defiance was a celebrity's calling card.

The turning point in Trump's pursuit of celebrity arrived in 2004 when the British producer Mark Burnett adapted his pioneering reality show *Survivor* to a business setting and called it *The Apprentice*. With Trump as the host and a catchy tagline, "You're fired!," the series became a ratings hit. In the end, Trump hosted *The Apprentice* and its spin-off, *The Celebrity Apprentice*, for a collective fourteen seasons. "Most of us knew he was a fake," one of the show's producers told the *New Yorker* in 2019. "He has just gone through I don't know how many bankruptcies. But we made him out to be the most important person in the world. It was like making the court jester the king."[13]

What propelled him were the same forces that Robert Putnam described in *Bowling Alone*. After the turn of the century, the internet and social media promoted individualism at the cost of the social capital all societies need. Celebrity worship self-selects for narcissistic males with a ravenous need for public attention. As he became increasingly famous, Trump began to monetize his fame with half of the profits from *The Apprentice* plus the gains from endorsements and product placements that included steaks, vodka, a board game, cologne, neckties, shirts, and casinos. Soon his name was on buildings, golf courses, a for-profit college, and an airline shuttle, most of which went bankrupt.

In 2010, Mark Burnett aimed his weapons of mass distraction at the American public again with Sarah Palin, the former vice presidential nominee who in 2008 had made politics about cultural identity. He created *Sarah Palin's Alaska*, a reality television show that ran for eight episodes in just a single season before it was canceled. But in translating presidential politics into a reality TV show, she gathered five million viewers and demonstrated to Donald Trump that there was nothing crazy about his continuing quest to do the opposite—turn his own reality show into presidential politics.

Meanwhile, with an additional boost from his "Mondays with Trump" segment on *Fox & Friends*, by the time the 2016 Republican primaries arrived, Trump was the only presold celebrity among the many candidates. Of the seventeen declared candidates, he was the only one with meaningful television exposure and who understood how tightly celebrities are embedded in the lives of the voters. There was nothing new about this for him. Trump had consistently used his visibility as a celebrity to promote his brand and his public career. What he uniquely realized was that people wanted unmediated access to the president, just as they now had with any other social media star.

Trump's 2015 announcement at the Trump Tower of his presidential candidacy mimicked the gaudy visuals and production values of *The Apprentice*. Like earlier celebrities from the nineteenth century, such as P. T. Barnum and Sarah Bernhardt, he did not pause at the edge of self-parody. If Trump could have had himself photographed in a coffin, as Sarah Bernhardt did, he would have done it to win attention and fame. "It may not be good for America, but it's damn good for CBS," said Les Moonves, the network's CEO at the time.[14]

Never again will a national election be so devoid of celebrities. If anything, the population of celebrities who have tested the political waters has only increased since the Trump presidency. In 2022, they included the following:

Dr. Mehmet Oz, the TV doctor, who lost his race for the US Senate in Pennsylvania after his former celebrity patron, Oprah Winfrey, endorsed John Fetterman

Dwayne "The Rock" Johnson, a professional wrestler and actor who in September 22 had 334 million Instagram followers and has expressed presidential ambitions

Matthew McConaughey, the actor who flirted with running for the Texas governorship and spoke with passion at the White House about the school shooting in Uvalde

Herschel Walker, the former NFL player who ran a competitive race for the US Senate in Georgia

J. D. Vance, the author of the best-seller *Hillbilly Elegy*, who won his first-ever campaign for the US Senate in Ohio

Caitlyn Jenner, the Olympian, reality-show star, and self-styled transgender rights activist whose bid to replace Governor Gavin Newsom in the California recall election failed dismally

What does the rise of celebrity candidates tell us about our politics? As analyst Chris Cillizza observed on CNN:

For Donald Trump, success on television is the only yardstick of success. When Trump endorsed TV doctor-entrepreneur Mehmet Oz in the 2022 Senate campaign in Pennsylvania, Trump explained, "I have known Dr. Oz for many years, as have many others, even if only through his very successful television show. He has lived with us through the screen and has always been popular, respected, and smart." At a rally in North Carolina, Trump elaborated, "When you're in television for eighteen years, that's like a poll. That means people like you." [15]

As Cillizza noted, Trump's support was based on the fact that Oz was on TV regularly for more than a decade. That made him famous. It also made him popular. "Trump likes famous, popular people who were on TV," Cillizza summarized. "Trump isn't endorsing Oz for any other reason. That's good enough for him. TV then is—and always has been—the way that Trump relates to the world. If it's on TV, it's real to Trump. And, if it's on TV for a long time—as he would often note his show *The Apprentice* was—then it (and the person behind it) must be good. . . . There's no part of his calculation to endorse Oz that dealt with whether the TV doctor would actually make a good senator."

What have we learned? First, that the celebrity politician has replaced community organizations. People who used to be bowling or working for their voting leagues are now at home watching TV or hunched over their smartphones on social media—likely both. Celebrities have stepped into the space vacated by civic engagement. This has allowed pop culture to be more democratic—more directly responsive to the taste of the masses—than ever before. But it has also elevated and empowered those celebrities who are most able to engage the greatest number of people. *Empowered* might be too strong a word, because these celebrities aren't so much leading their millions of followers as being led by them. To be popular to so many, so successfully, for so long, you must necessarily appeal to and, in appealing, reinforce your followers' popular notions.

Second, that the art of governing is at risk. If your job as an entertainer has been to appeal to as many of the cultural commonplaces of your audience as possible, it would run against your nature, even if you are now a politician trying to solve problems, to look beyond their commonplace political assumptions for answers. To do so would to be to risk alienating an audience that has, since you declared your candidacy, become your political base—an audience that you're the world expert at reading and keeping satisfied. So, instead of taking professional advice, you start giving them what they want to hear, and not what is necessarily good for the country—true whether your audience is conservative or liberal. While the typical politician risks taking advice from fairly obscure and potentially unpopular experts—economists, academics, policy analysts—you use your skill at appealing to huge audiences to excite and affirm what your base thinks.

While these appeals will likely make you a good candidate, they're unlikely to help you solve the complex problems that imperil the very complex system of government you must head when you win the election. The social media savvy celebrity who runs for office (and which celebrity isn't social media savvy these days?) is a populist in spirit and in practice, perfectly attuned to the will of the people. While it may seem harmless to be attuned to entertainment that directly appeals to popular tastes, there's lots of potential for harm when this highly democratic culture uses the vessel of celebrity to infect politics with ratings-tested policies—that is to say, when it's no longer ideas for songs, cover art, and performances that arise from the Twitter feeds of followers but ideas for executive orders, legislative solutions, and trade agreements. This seems to be the natural drift of things because the celebrity-politicians are highly attuned to their base in the broadest terms. What they are less sensitive to are the opinions and needs of voices in the back of the room and the ideas from the historical margins that need and deserve a hearing.

Finally, we must return to the vexing question of the distinction between causation and correlation. Is the arrival of celebrities in politics caused by low social capital, as explored in the previous chapter? Or are both caused by a third variable, such as the dominance of name recognition produced by the internet? In any case, celebrity seems to have escaped the picture frame we once kept it in. To all of our confusion and dismay, celebrity has become the loudest voice in the room.

CHAPTER 9

THE HUMAN COSTS OF CELEBRITY

Didn't you used to be somebody famous?"

So much is packed into that sentence. Certainly, the evanescence of celebrity, its rewards and recognition, is all too fleeting. So are the inevitable personal wounds wrapped into the celebrity package. One question can take away what was so hard-earned.

Being a celebrity has become a profession in itself with defined skills and benefits. It can tell us something about who we are, what we value. But what about when the cheering stops? If a celebrity doesn't compel the public's full attention, can they be said to exist?

Not long after I became the editor of *People*, I went to the Academy Awards—and learned more than I wanted to about the then divisive machinery of celebrity. While waiting for the televised Oscars ceremony to begin, I noticed that the audience was breathless, glamorous, and entirely white. Then I noticed a scrum of equally well-dressed people patiently standing in the outside aisles flanking the rows of seats.

"Who are they?" I asked.

"Oh, those are the seat fillers."

Seat fillers? The seat fillers turned out to be the people who are assigned to sit in any seats left glaringly empty if an Oscar winner went to the stage, or to the bathroom. So if the TV cameras again panned over the audience, the vacated seats were still pleasingly filled.

The seat fillers were also all white.

Who were these lucky few? They turned out to be friends and family of well-connected members of the Academy of Motion Picture Arts and Sciences and ABC Television. They were not celebrities; they just looked like them. The upshot? Even when Hollywood had the opportunity to fake diversity, it chose not to.

This should not have been a surprise. When Hattie McDaniel was nominated for an Academy Award for playing Mammy in *Gone with the Wind*, she was not allowed to stay at the Ambassador Hotel or sit with the rest of the cast at the Cocoanut Grove ballroom. When Paul Robeson dared express his political views, he was followed by the FBI. Before he could make his breakthrough film appearance, in *Blackboard Jungle*, Sidney Poitier was asked by the House Un-American Activities Committee to sign a loyalty oath denouncing both Robeson and the actor-activist Canada Lee. When Eartha Kitt dared to criticize the Vietnam War at LBJ's White House, she was ostracized. They were all guilty of Speaking Out While Black.

The evidence was everywhere—and even worse than we knew. The following year, *People* did a cover story that took note of the fact that of the 166 nominees for the 1996 Academy Awards, only one was Black (for a live-action short film). The magazine further documented that of the academy's 5,043 members, fewer than 200 were Black (3.9 percent). It was no better with the Directors Guild of America (2.3 percent), the Writers Guild of America (2.6 percent), or stagehand unions (2 percent). In other words, even though Black Americans were 13 percent of the population and fully 25 percent of moviegoers,

Hollywood did not reflect their lives on-screen or offer them the traditional route to celebrity. As I knew it would, the cover story, called "Hollywood Blackout," bombed at the newsstands. It took another twenty years for the Oscars So White protests to arrive in 2016—and even then Hollywood tried to hunker down and wait for it to blow over.

Black women have been hit particularly hard by racial disparities in the celebrity system. Musical performers like Marian Anderson and Josephine Baker faced humiliating setbacks early in their careers. It was no different in this century for pop singer Janet Jackson. When she joined Justin Timberlake for the halftime show of the 2004 Super Bowl in Houston to perform "Rock Your Body," Timberlake either inadvertently or deliberately exposed her breast—and thereby generated "Nipplegate" and the most searched-for person and term of 2004 and 2005. YouTube's founder Jawed Karim later credited the "wardrobe malfunction" for providing the impetus to start his video-sharing website. Jackson was blamed for staging the incident, and her career went into a prolonged decline. Timberlake, who may well have staged it, emerged unscathed.

The vulnerability of Black entertainers in public settings was vividly on display when Will Smith delivered his notorious slap to Chris Rock at the 2022 Oscars. The spectacle of one Black man hitting another one, on live TV, dominated the nation's news for a week.

Smith justified his action as in defense of his wife, Jada Pinkett Smith, a fact not lost on many Black women who saw it and appreciated it, though some found it paternalistic. Unlike Hattie McDaniel or Eartha Kitt, the Smith family had been able to monetize their fame. Westbrook Studios, the production arm of the media company the family started in 2019, was valued at $600 million in 2022. Smith's public apology, an act required of all misbehaving celebrities, may have limited the potential damage.[1]

Today, amid the profusion of defiant celebrities generated by social media and the internet, the cloistered world of Janet

Jackson and Justin Timberlake seems almost quaint. In the entertainment world, the process has been democratized, if not equalized. And as we've previously noted, virtually anyone can become famous with enough patience and enough Twitter followers. The hand of redemption awaits many women who have been through hellish experiences. Monica Lewinsky, Pamela Anderson, Lorena Bobbitt, Tonya Harding, Elizabeth Holmes, Marcia Clark, and Martha Mitchell were all once the objects of public scorn and have since told (or sold) their stories publicly with the promise of redemption.[2]

On one hand, this theoretically opens the halls of celebrity to minorities and generations of left-outs—although the pressures to succeed remain powerful as does the fear of failure. On the other hand, almost everyone who finds fame is at risk. They may suffer from the very real diagnosis of what is known as *acquired situational narcissism.*

No, there is not yet a pill for that. Dr. Robert B. Millman has defined acquired situational narcissism (ASN) as a condition in which those in high positions of power, such as movie stars, politicians, and professional athletes, develop narcissistic traits as a result of their fame.[3] ASN is a multifaceted personality trait that combines grandiosity, attention seeking, an unrealistically inflated self-view, a need for that self-view to be continuously reinforced, and a general lack of regard for others—sound familiar?

Narcissism can lead people to seek out fame, but ASN develops after achieving success, sometimes intensifying narcissistic tendencies that were already present. ASN is fed by attention from others. However, individuals with ASN tend to be high-profile celebrities, so the attention they receive is necessarily more intense and constantly reinforced by their employees, the media, and of course by their fans and followers.[4]

"The narcissist depends on others to validate his self-esteem. He cannot live without an admiring audience," Christopher Lasch wrote in *The Culture of Narcissism.* "The mass media, with their cult of celebrity, and their attempt to surround it with glamour and excitement, have made Americans a nation of fans, moviegoers. The media give substance to and thus intensify narcissistic dreams of fame and glory, encouraging the common man to identify himself with the stars and to hate 'the herd,' and make it more and more difficult for him to accept the banality of everyday existence."[5]

The result is that fame is destructive. Over the years, the escape route many stars have used is drugs. The list of celebrity deaths from suicide and drugs is long and continually updated— Elvis Presley, Judy Garland, Marilyn Monroe, Jim Morrison, Janis Joplin, Jimi Hendrix, Lenny Bruce, Freddy Prinze, Whitney Houston, John Belushi, River Phoenix, Michael Jackson, Anthony Bourdain, Kate Spade, and Robin Williams.[6]

Like many celebrities, Williams could feel the damage in his own life. In one long-ago episode of *Mork & Mindy*, he wonders why celebrity is prized. "Don't you understand that a star is just a big ball of glowing hot gas?" he asks. "He's just an ordinary human being that's been hyped by an advertising campaign." Continuing to speak on camera in his role as Mork, Williams memorably summarizes what he had learned about fame. " 'When you're a celebrity,' he says, 'everybody wants a piece of you, sir. Unless you can say no, you'll have nothing left.' " Williams (aka Mork) concludes that the price was just too much for some people to take, " 'and to be honest, sir, some of them can't take it.' "[7]

Mork's sentiments do not sound that different from those of Jean-Jacques Rousseau, who, two hundred years earlier, complained that his celebrity was a burden that condemned him to live "more alone in the middle of Paris than Robinson [Crusoe] on his island, and sequestered from the intercourse with men by the crowd itself, eager to surround him in order to prevent him from allying with anyone."[8]

The risks contemporary celebrities face has been studied, notably by Mark Bellis and his colleagues, who attempted to test the truism that rock stars in particular play hard and die early. (The results were published in a paper called "Elvis to Eminem: Quantifying the Price of Fame Through Early Mortality of European and North American Rock and Pop Stars," in the *Journal of Epidemiology & Community Health*.)[9] The researchers measured the survival rates of musicians who had performed on any album in the all-time top one thousand albums from the genres of rock, punk, rap, R&B, electronica, and New Age.

What did they discover? That in their early years of fame, both North American and European pop stars experience significantly higher mortality (more than 1.7 times) than demographically matched populations in the USA and UK, respectively. But after twenty-five years of fame, relative mortality in European (but not North American) pop stars begins to return to population levels.

The researchers concluded that pop stars can suffer high levels of stress in environments where alcohol and drugs are widely available, leading to health-damaging risk behavior. Moreover, their behavior can also influence would-be stars and devoted fans. As they put it, "Collaborations between health and music industries should focus on improving both pop star health and their image as role models to wider populations."[10]

The interactions of the media with celebrities can be unpredictable. I had a hand in one embarrassing incident during my time at *People*. Late at night, I was closing a story about the actor Abe Vigoda, well known from the TV show *Barney Miller* and from *The Godfather*, in which he played the dour mobster Tessio. When I saw Vigoda's name in print, perhaps remembering his saturnine presence from *The Godfather*, I thought, "Well, he's dead now." So I wrote into the story, "the late Abe Vigoda."

In fact, Vigoda was alive. He called a press conference to prove it and posed in a coffin holding a copy of *People*. He lived another thirty-four years, I think to spite me. He died in 2016 at age ninety-four. His obit in the *New York Times* mentioned this sorry episode in the first paragraph.

I often wonder if I thought he was dead because his time of great celebrity had passed. In other words, the incident was an illustration of how easy it is to conclude that if someone is no longer in the media circus, they must have died.

Sadly, the injuries experienced by most celebrities are not so reversible. Charles Figley of Tulane University has devoted a lifetime to the study of individual and social trauma, including with celebrities. In one study, he mailed two hundred questionnaires to names randomly selected from a list of the public's top-ranked celebrities. Using the information gathered from the fifty-one responses, Figley compiled a list of the primary sources of stress for celebrities and their families, as well as their reactions and solutions. Most of the questionnaires were completed by the celebrities, the rest were completed by a spouse, friend, or adult child of the celebrity. The top ten stressors, in order, were these:

- the media
- critics
- threatening letters/calls
- the lack of privacy
- the constant monitoring of their lives
- worry about career plunges
- stalkers
- lack of security
- curious fans
- worries about their children's lives being disrupted.

Perhaps surprisingly, especially given their relative wealth, the life expectancy of celebrities is shorter than that of people who do not have to cope with the slings and arrows of fame. In a sample of one hundred stars, Jib Fowles, a professor of media studies at the University of Houston, found that stars on average do indeed die much younger than the rest of the US population.[11] "The average age at death for Americans was 71.9 years, while for the stars it was 58.7—a full 13.2 years younger," he reported. Even more disturbing, Fowles found there was "a remarkable differential [in the average age of death] between the sexes." Female celebrities fared much worse, dying on average at age 54.3, an astonishing 21.5 years earlier than the average American woman, who died at 75.8. Fowles concluded that the stresses built into the job of performing as a celebrity are far more hazardous for women than for men. Ominously, Fowles's study was conducted in 1992, well before the arrival of the pressure-cooker environment of the internet and social media.

Celebrities are highly aware of who and what the media wants them to be, down the finest detail. As Kenneth Gergen writes, in *Rational Being: Beyond Self and Community*, "We are bombarded, for example, with advertisements regarding the most desirable body shape, clothing styles, color of the teeth, texture of the hair and so on. The media inform us of what is 'in' in the way of music, books, restaurants, film, and wine. Everywhere we encounter the 'top 100,' 'the top ten,' and 'number one.'"[12]

Here is Eric Clapton: "All we want to do is be left alone to make music but because we are 'rock stars' a whole different set of expectancies are thrust upon us. That we have instant opinions about everything, that we should set an example to the youth of today by making public statements about drugs, that we should dress and behave like the freaks we are supposed to be."[13]

No wonder celebrities named the media as their number-one stressor in Charles Figley's survey. There is essentially an unspoken Faustian bargain between the celebrities and the media. If the celebrities cooperate with the media (and the more they feed the media's needs, the bigger they become), they hold on to their fame and fortune, but at the cost of their individuality, their privacy, even their independence. And the more famous they become, the more vulnerable they become. Howard Bragman, the Hollywood crisis management guru, calls it "the piñata syndrome." As he puts it, "It's really about the media. They're only lifting you up so that they can take sticks and beat you and see what comes out."[14]

What this amounts to is that our addiction to fame has become a key component of the American dream—but one that betrays us. F. Scott Fitzgerald previewed it in his judgment about the wealthy Buchanans in *The Great Gatsby*: "They were careless people, Tom and Daisy—they smashed up things and creatures and then retreated back into their money or their vast carelessness or whatever it was that kept them together, and let other people clean up the mess they had made."

The question we are left with is whether the rise of celebrity addiction caused the breakdown of our civic assets, or whether both are correlated with a third factor, such as the impact of the internet and social media since the turn of the century.

Some rare celebrities have been able to navigate their way through the Scylla and Charybdis of celebrity and social media by fiercely retaining their own identities. One is Janet Mock, the writer, television host, director, producer, and transgender rights activist. Her memoir *Redefining Realness* honestly and openly invited the world into the life of a multiracial trans woman. As she movingly concludes:

> For so much of my life … I was steadily reaching in the dark across a chasm that separated who I was and who I thought I should be. Somewhere along the way I grew weary of grasping at possible selves, just out of reach. I put my arms down and wrapped them around me. I began healing by embracing myself through the foreboding darkness until the sunrise shone on my face. Eventually I emerged, and surrendered to the brilliance, discovering truth, beauty, and peace that was already mine.[15]

CHAPTER 10

SWIMMING WITH NARCISSUS

Over the past quarter century, celebrity emerged from the sideshows to occupy the center ring in America. Our children aspire to it at the costs of their happiness and the health of their communities.

To understand this, it helps to return to the lessons the Greeks and Romans gave us in the form of their gods. For the Greeks, the gods were celebrities. The psychic mechanism the Greeks projected onto their gods is the same one that everyday citizens encounter with our celebrities. One of the primary characteristics they share is the particular aura that surrounds both gods and celebrities, Rudolf Otto's *numinosity*. They are seen as larger than life and endowed with special qualities. They are group projections and carry enormous collective emotion— the innate human yearning for religious, supercharged, or numinous experience. That same collective emotion that created the gods of the Greeks is now creating celebrities—whether they are seen as good angels or bad angels. We need them to worship. When a celebrity walks into a restaurant, our forks freeze in the air.

In his prescient 2009 book, *Empire of Illusion: The End of Literacy and the Triumph of Spectacle*, Chris Hedges does not

spare us the dire consequences of our intoxication and possession with celebrity:

> Celebrity culture plunges us into a moral void. No one has
> any worth beyond his or her appearance, usefulness, or abil-
> ity to *succeed*. The highest achievements in a celebrity culture
> are wealth, sexual conquest, and fame. It does not matter how
> these are obtained. These values . . . are illusory. They are hol-
> low. They leave us chasing vapors. They urge us toward a life
> of narcissistic self-absorption. They tell us that existence is
> to be centered on the practices and desires of the self rather
> than the common good. The ability to lie and manipulate
> others is held up as the highest good. The cult of self domi-
> nates our cultural landscape. This cult has within it the classic
> traits of the psychopaths: superficial charm, grandiosity, and
> self-importance; a need for constant stimulation, a penchant
> for lying, deception and manipulation, and the inability to
> feel remorse or guilt. It is the misguided belief that personal
> style and personal advancements, mistaken for individual-
> ism, are the same as democratic equality. We have a right, in
> the cult of the self, to get whatever we desire. We can do any-
> thing, even belittle and destroy those around us, including
> our friends, to make money, to be happy, and to become fa-
> mous. Once fame and wealth are achieved, they become their
> own justification, their own morality. How one gets there is
> irrelevant. Once you get there, those questions are no longer
> asked.[1]

But there are distinctions. In ancient Greece, one never became a hero while alive. It was a status bestowed on one only in
death. It was a highly honored status and not for the living. In
a way, the Greeks knew a lot more than we do because they understood that you do not conflate the gods and goddesses with
mortals. There could be communication, even sex, between

gods and goddesses and mortals—and there were certainly influences on human behavior by the gods and goddesses.

But they understood the difference between mortality and immortality. Over the last two thousand years, we got rid of the gods and goddesses, but they still can be understood as projections of the human psyche. We continue to invest deep reverence onto celebrities, but we have lost the feel for the separation of mortal and immortal.

Narcissus is an essential god in Greek mythology. Ovid tells us in the *Metamorphoses* that Narcissus was a handsome youth who fell in love with his own reflected image in a river. Unable to leave the allure of his image, he eventually realized that his love could not be reciprocated, and he melted away from the fire of passion burning inside him, eventually drowning and turning into a gold and white flower.

What has Narcissus given us in America? The contempt of the rest of the world. In the academic journals, study after study has found that both Americans and non-Americans alike perceive other Americans as the most narcissistic people in the world, reflecting the belief that "the typical American is grandiose, callous, and self-centered."[2] This opinion comes from both American college students and citizens of other world regions.

The idea that American culture is narcissistic is not new. It dates to Tom Wolfe's famous article "The 'Me' Decade and the Third Great Awakening," in *New York Magazine* (1976), and Christopher Lasch's *The Culture of Narcissism* (1979). Only recently have researchers tried to study our national character to find the mechanism that made us this way. Studies show that narcissistic individuals are more likely to use social media platforms, tweet more frequently, have more followers on social media, and post more selfies. Americans have a larger presence on social media than the people in any other nation. For example, 76.9 million Americans use Twitter, compared to 58.95 million in Japan and 23.6 million in India.[3]

For celebrities in particular, narcissism is an occupational hazard. Until recently, most of what we know about celebrities has been anecdotal, filtered through interviews and magazine articles. Moreover, access to celebrities is generally carefully controlled by their agents and publicists, making them one of the most widely exposed but least understood groups in society.

In their study on narcissism and celebrity for UCLA, Mark Young and Drew Pinsky used the Narcissistic Personality Inventory (NPI) to compare a large sample of celebrities to cohorts of MBA students and the general public. They found that "celebrities were significantly more narcissistic" than the other groups.[4] Contrary to findings in the population at large, in which men are more narcissistic than women, female celebrities were found to be significantly more narcissistic than their male counterparts.

Then they dug in deeper, comparing four different types of celebrities using a series of linear contrasts. Reality television personalities had the highest narcissism scores, followed by comedians, actors, and musicians. Both reality television personalities and actors had significantly higher narcissism scores than musicians, although the scores for actors, comedians, and reality TV personalities did not differ significantly. Breaking their characteristics down into component characteristics of narcissism—authority, exhibitionism, superiority, entitlement, exploitativeness, self-sufficiency, and vanity—a further analysis showed that for authority, comedians, reality TV personalities, and actors scored significantly higher than musicians. Regarding exhibitionism, both actors and comedians scored significantly higher than musicians. For superiority, comedians scored higher than musicians and actors. The results for vanity showed that actors, reality TV personalities, and musicians scored higher than comedians, and that reality TV personalities and actors scored higher than musicians. On exploitativeness, comedians scored higher than musicians and actors, whereas reality TV personalities also scored significantly higher than musicians and actors.

Musicians appear to be the least narcissistic celebrity group. They did not score higher than any of the other categories of celebrities in any dimension. On the other hand, comedians had the highest average scores on five of the component scales—authority, exhibitionism, superiority, entitlement, and exploitativeness—and scored higher than musicians in all of these dimensions. Reality TV personalities and actors evince the highest overall average NPI score, and reality TV personalities scored higher than actors on exploitativeness.

As the researchers observed,

> Reality television has provided an outlet for narcissistic individuals, many with limited abilities, to believe that they can succeed in the entertainment industry. This desire to enter the industry may be fueled by the types of fantasy feelings of success, power and glory that narcissists seem to exhibit. It could also be the case that the producers of reality television shows have reasons for picking the most narcissistic contestants. First, as the literature shows, narcissists are liked initially [. . .]; thus, casting agents and producers may be drawn to hire them. Second, from an audience standpoint, narcissists tend to create drama and, thus, are entertaining to watch, especially in competitive situations.

What is important and perhaps counterintuitive to remember is that, as Young and Pinsky note, "Narcissism is not a by-product of celebrity, but a primary motivating force that drives people to *become* celebrities."

More recently, in 2017, Courtland S. Hyatt and a group of collaborators attempted to demonstrate that the icons of American celebrity are so demonstrably narcissistic that their omnipresence could have brainwashed people around the world to believe that *all* Americans are that way. The researchers devised a study to determine if exposure to American celebrities alone would lead the participants to rate Americans in general higher on the measurable traits of narcissism.[5]

How would they do it? The researchers would expose one group of eighty-six participants from a large Southern university to a dose of popular culture in the pages of celebrity-based magazines. Specifically, they would read *People* and *Lifestyle* magazines for fifteen minutes. The other group would read the celebrity-neutral *Consumer Reports* and *Scientific American*. The hypothesis was that those participants in the celebrity-magazine reading group would later give higher ratings to Americans for narcissism—thus supporting the idea that the reputation of Americans for rampant narcissism was driven by celebrity role models.

To my surprise—and infinite relief—the participants who read *People* and *Lifestyle* did not run screaming from the room, nor did they rate Americans as more narcissistic than did the readers of *Scientific American* and *Consumer Reports*. Undeterred, the researchers wondered if the fifteen-minute reading sessions were too short to make an impression on participants, and they speculated about surveying magazine subscribers or habitual viewers of reality television shows in the future.[6]

How we imagine and respond to fame tells us as much about ourselves as it does about celebrities and heroes. Not surprisingly, artists were among the first to register the iconography of celebrity. Early American painters like John Trumbull and Charles Willson Peale painted not just heroes but also the events that made them heroic—Washington at Trenton or Washington at Princeton. The spirit is of the heroic moment benefiting a larger community. Think of Jacques-Louis David's *Napoleon Crossing the Alps*. George Caleb Bingham's paintings in the American West during the Early Republic envisioned the common man as an exemplar of democratic values in works like *The County Election* and *The Verdict of the People* (albeit with women and Native Americans pointedly crowded into the margins). If you walk through the National Portrait Gallery at the Smithsonian these days, however, you will find not only US presidents in our Parthenon but also Shirley MacLaine, Pete Sampras, John Travolta, Brad Pitt, Oprah Winfrey, and Ellen DeGeneres.

It took Andy Warhol to investigate the individualistic side of celebrity, starting with his silk-screened meditations on public figures like O. J. Simpson, Muhammad Ali, and Marilyn Monroe. When Warhol's 1964 silk screen of Monroe's face, *Shot Sage Blue Marilyn*, sold for $195 million in 2022, it set a then-record for the price of a single American work of art at auction. This artistic critique of celebrity culture was joined by works from others, such as James Rosenquist and Jeff Koons.

Lady Gaga once prided herself on her special stature. In her 2013 hit "Applause," she sings, "One second I'm a kunst / Then suddenly the kunst is me." Lady Gaga here plays on the transformation of celebrity from "a kunst" (in German, a piece of art) into "the kunst" (the art). Celebrities haven't only become pieces of art, Gaga seems to be saying, but also *the* only art. As if to clarify her meaning, she then sings, "Pop culture was in art / Now, art's in pop culture in me." In a great reversal, the "me" of the celebrity, once generated and contained by "art" and "culture," now comprises both. Not even the greatest art is safe: on the cover of her album *ARTPOP*, Botticelli's *Birth of Venus* appears, but only underneath the image of Gaga Herself.

Art depends on the wrappings of celebrity to make its way. It's not simply that the novels of Tolstoy and Cervantes get a sales boost when Oprah's imprimatur is on the cover, but also that *Hamlet* makes real money only as a vehicle for Benedict Cumberbatch. It takes legions of celebrities assembled at the Met Gala to draw the nation's gaze for a single evening to the place that holds one of the world's great art collections.

Celebrity has impacted even the way we talk. Consider first the vocabulary that typically surrounds the descriptions of heroes. It is Homeric; heroes gird their loins with words like *valor, courage, sacrifice, fortitude, daring, gallantry, honor.*

Celebrities, on the other hand, dine on a thinner gruel: *ensemble, promotion, gossip, diva, flaunt, cachet, fashion, splurge, tabloid.* This is a vocabulary that is temporary, provisional, passive, and always reversible. Some of the chosen vocabulary is transparently chosen for its publicity value.

Take *feud*, a word increasingly associated with millennial celebrities like Katy Perry and Taylor Swift, who publicly dislike each other and write songs, pull publicity stunts, and start Twitter wars over it.

Or the term *creative team*, referring to the personal stylists and marketers that some pop stars employ to curate and fashion their appearance and brand.

Fandom refers to the fans of a particular celebrity (usually but not exclusively female). These fandoms usually acquire their own branded names: Beyoncé has her Beyhive; Ariana Grande has her Arianators.

The metaphors that surround celebrity culture are instructive. The often-contrarian critic Joseph Epstein writes: "Celebrity at this moment in America is epidemic, and it's spreading fast, sometime seeming as if nearly everyone has got it."[7]

In other words, it's a disease. It's contagious, like, say, COVID-19. Writing in the *British Journal of Psychology*, Lynn E. McCutcheon claimed that one-third of Americans suffer "from celebrity worship syndrome" and that "most of the rest of us [Americans] are at risk of developing the condition."[8]

However, the prospect of confession and redemption, even for stars who've broken the law or transgressed codes of conduct, proves their fixed and unassailable status in American society. Americans can get rid of their spouses, their elected officials, and their presidents more easily than we can dislodge a celebrity from the public consciousness.

Perhaps they're largely unassailable because of all the organizations and businesses that have a stake in them—certain celebrities, it seems, are too big to fail. Even the failure of death cannot destroy the biggest stars, who continue to make huge amounts of money for their estates and for those invested in them: Michael Jackson died in 2009, but despite credible stories of his sexual abuse of children, his estate earned $825 million in 2016.[9]

With their visibility in their chosen markets, and armed with a tonnage of viewers and followers and algorithms, social influencers have carved out a market so impactful and beholden to advertisers that the Federal Trade Commission issued warnings to them almost from the start.

Over time, the periodic table of celebrities, with Hollywood at the apex, gave way to a less organized taxonomy, populated by real people who morphed into reality television and social media stars. These were the boom years of celebrity, and as in any time of irrational exuberance, no one wanted to take away the punch bowl and turn out the lights.

The upshot is that there is no longer a natural aristocracy of talent and charisma that establishes the value of fame; it is an aristocracy of numbers—the calculus of followers, likes, friends, and downloads.

The algorithms allow marketers to tease out all the behavioral tics and purchasing patterns of the users. In the eyes of the algorithms, we are a nation of consumers.

The irony is that, as celebrity culture has become increasingly democratized by social media, American society itself has never felt so unequal, so ossified, so undemocratic. The users of Twitter and Instagram who see the people they chose to follow achieve fame and fortune look around and do not see a similarly robust democracy operating in politics. That is to say, our political leaders (with the exception of Donald Trump) have been slow to apply celebrity rules to workings of American republicanism.

Which makes the extraordinary rise of Volodymyr Zelenskyy from TV sitcom star to become the president of Ukraine all the more extraordinary. The man tellingly described as "the Tom Hanks of Ukraine" became its Winston Churchill.[10] Zelenskyy reversed the typical, well-worn path from statesman to celebrity to show that a man of courage and principle can win simply by demonstrating his character, no matter what the personal risk.

Zelenskyy used the tools of celebrity to propel himself into hero and leader. In his satirical sitcom *Servant of the People*, Zelenskyy played a modest teacher, Vasily Petrovych Goloborodko, whose on-camera tirade against state corruption leads to his winning the presidency—eerily presaging Zelenskyy's own real-life triumph in 2019.

It did not take long for the academic studies to follow Zelenskyy's path. In their 2022 study for the *European Journal of Communication*, Nataliya Roman and her colleagues examined the concept of "fictional framing" in *Servant of the People* as well as in TV dramas like *The West Wing* and *Veep* to find out how similar the shows were in portraying presidents and how much they blur the distinctions between reality and entertainment. Their conclusion was that Volodymyr Zelenskyy and the creators of *Servant of the People* referenced real problems in Ukrainian government such as widespread corruption, poorly maintained infrastructure, and delays in payments to state workers. As they wrote,

> These mentions make the show even more relatable and believable for Ukrainian audiences and likely contribute[d] to the success of the sitcom and to Zelenskyy's victory in the 2019 presidential election. . . . By using humor to frame Zelenskyy's fictional presidential character as "principled," viewers of the character may have transferred positive feelings for the Goloborodko character to Zelenskyy the actor in his bid for election, equating his character's reformist behaviours with the types of behaviours Zelenskyy would engage in as president.[11]

The study's findings have relevance beyond Ukraine because the number of television celebrities running for political office is increasing globally. A prominent example is Jimmy Morales, who starred in a television comedy show in Guatemala for fourteen years before serving as president of the country from 2016 to 2020.

It is clear that the cult of celebrity is intrinsically tied to mass communications. We can date it to the almost simultaneous introductions of social media and the smartphone around 2006. Constant media exposure creates a feedback loop. Because people are interested in celebrities, media cover them, and because they are constantly in the media, they attract more fans. Thus scaled up, public visibility becomes a form of mythology, part of our collective memory, part of generational imprinting.

To date, most of the data about public behavior gathered on social media remains in the possession of the platforms themselves, available for profit making and influence trading. It is out of the hands of anyone who wishes to use it to rebuild social capital in America.

No wonder the public remains deeply ambivalent about the influence of celebrities on our lives. On one hand, we admire and emulate celebrities and seek the rewards they have gained. It's as if we're not trying to keep up with the Joneses anymore; we're trying to dance with the stars. This has left the public bewildered and disoriented about the sources of celebrity and its true value. Celebrity is a source of prestige and power yet today it is also an object of scorn, treated with suspicion and disdain. Among celebrities, pop singers are particularly prone to feel the slings and arrows of fame. David Bowie waxed ironic in his 1975 single "Fame" that "What you get is no tomorrow / What you need you have to borrow." Some singers such as Kurt Cobain, Lorde, Whitney Houston, and Billie Eilish have similarly bemoaned their fates.

Madonna is well aware of this distinction. "Fame is a by-product," she says. "Fame is something that should happen because you do work that speaks to people and people want to know about your work. Unfortunately, the personality of people has taken over from the work and the artistry and it's this thing now that stands on its own. I don't think one should ever aspire to being famous."[12]

To return to what the Greeks knew, heroic qualities were those that people prayed for and were thankful for. A hero was chosen by the gods but existed for the benefit of us all. This would suggest that fame, even in this early heroic form, has always been thought to stem from and be mediated and regulated by a higher power. The fame of the earliest celebrities similarly derived from higher sources that, while not divine, had certainly condescended to select and elevate them: museum curators who chose to feature their sculptures and oils, publishers who picked their books for printing, movie studio heads who cast them in films, recording studios that produced their albums, and popular publications (and yes, their editors, people like me) that decided to expose their work and personalities to mass audiences.

The internet and social media have made fame all the more omnipresent and profitable and often cost us our honor and our loyalty to community. Where do we go from here? The question before us now, then, is the one that beguiled Narcissus. If we gaze into the water, will we see the reflections of narcissists in our midst? Or will we learn to put our definition of celebrity into a worldview that rejects the fraudulent and embraces the likes of Volodymyr Zelenskyy, who moved from a fictional world into a factual one with integrity and commitment and proved his mettle under the worst circumstances?

The lesson we need is still in front of us.

CHAPTER 11

STORIES CELEBRITIES TELL

What is the life story of a famous person? Who tells it? Who listens to it? Why?

Those questions have always been with us. The literary tradition itself dates to Julius Caesar's *The Gallic Wars* and Saint Augustine's *Confessions*. Today celebrities write their own stories —or pay someone to do it for them. Nearly half of the bestsellers on the *New York Times* hardcover nonfiction list in recent years have been written by celebrities. Faced with reading them, we might smile brightly or grit our teeth, but we sit up straight and hope for the best.

There are common themes that emerge in celebrity memoirs and autobiographies. Dan P. McAdams strove to identify them in his book *The Stories We Live By.* For McAdams, someone's life story goes hand in hand with the creation of a "personal myth."[1] A personal myth "is not an exercise in narcissistic delusion, or a paranoid attempt to establish oneself as God. Instead, defining the self through myth may be seen as an ongoing act of psychological and social *responsibility*. Because our world can no longer tell us who we are and how we should live, we must figure it out on our own. The making of a personal myth is a psychosocial quest." As McAdams puts it, "To create a personal myth is to fashion a history of the self."[2]

Memoirs and motion pictures are two of the most prominent ways to chronicle celebrity stories—both operate in the mainstream, both transform a life into a narrative, and both strive to create a personal myth in one way or another. In their original incarnations, celebrities from Hollywood's Golden Age wrote bodacious stories that were full of name-dropping, bragging, and innuendos. More recently, celebrity biographies take the form of a redemption narrative. Now the celebrities conquer challenge after challenge—domineering parents, substance abuse, struggles with sexual identity, and sexual assaults.

Fiction writers have also attempted to diagnose the inner workings of celebrity. Most such attempts have a certain evanescence. We think of Fitzgerald's Jay Gatsby, a celebrity in his rarefied social world always yearning for the unattainable Daisy. One of the earliest and most prominent such novels is now all but forgotten. *The Celebrity*, published in 1898, was the satirical first novel by the massively popular historical novelist Winston Churchill (no relation to the British prime minister).[3]

The American Churchill was probably the most popular novelist in America during the first quarter of the twentieth century in terms of book sales. His books constantly appeared on America's bestseller lists, listed in ten of the years between 1899 and 1917. But following this period of widespread readership, Churchill's relevance quickly diminished to the point where he very rarely appears in modern scholarship.[4]

The Celebrity is an outlier among Churchill's books; it is the only one explicitly about celebrity and fame and is written in a comedic tone that is somewhat distinct from his usual polemical voice. In Churchill's telling, the unnamed Celebrity is an unprincipled writer who assumes false identities and is revealed to be an extraordinary hypocrite who proposes to two women without any intention of marrying either of them. He freely admits to his hypocrisy and defends himself, asking,

"How many lawyers believe in their own arguments?" In the climax of the book, the Celebrity is exposed as a liar and humiliated.

Churchill's novel gives us an insight into popular attitudes about celebrity in the Gilded Age. In his telling, it is the excesses committed by the famous themselves that are at the root of America's problem with celebrities—that is, it's the fault of the famous, rather than the fault of the fans or the press. In virtually all contemporary scholarly work about *The Celebrity*, the Celebrity is universally understood to be an unsympathetic figure. Literary critic Warren Titus observes that "his foppishness, his insincerity, and his buoyant egotism are sources of annoyance," and American literature scholar Michele K. Troy calls him "a self-satisfied opportunist who cultivates his eccentricity to gain fame, money, and romance."[5]

The plot of the book is that the man called the Celebrity writes his own novel-within-a-novel called *The Sybarites*, which features a rich, wildly popular libertine who comes to realize that his hedonistic attitudes and tendency to break hearts are hurting those around him. In the turning point of *The Sybarites*, the libertine "reflects on a misspent and foolish life," and the reader is explicitly told "this, mind you, is where his character starts to develop." Seeing his error, he vows to live what is essentially the opposite life of the Celebrity, a life of "usefulness and seclusion" while staying faithful to his wife.

The "real" Celebrity, despite directly seeing the amount of difficulty he brings to those around him, has no such revelation and remains a celebrity even in the last paragraph of the novel, where he "is still writing books of a high moral tone and unapproachable principle, and his popularity is undiminished."[6] The Celebrity, at every possible moment, cynically acts for his own benefit and for the sake of increasing the positive attention surrounding him, without much care as to how it impacts anyone else, and is unable or unwilling to change his motivation. Churchill sees celebrity as a seduction—something that induces an absolute change in character and egotism with no possibility of redemption.

The consolidation of the self into the celebrity image is reflected by Churchill's decision to never name the fictional Celebrity by his "real" name, only ever referring to him as "the Celebrity" or by the name of the person whose identity the Celebrity has stolen, Charles Wrexell Allen. Churchill's refusal to reveal the name for the Celebrity is itself a comment on the nature of fame and recognizability. When someone becomes a celebrity, their name becomes widely known and associated with their public persona. From then on, when they meet someone, their name is immediately recognized and they are already known as their persona before they can even begin forming a relationship in earnest, meaning that now their name means nothing other than their celebrity persona.

There is little nuance to *The Celebrity*; the protagonist generally remains motivated by his public image first, followed by his hedonism, and seems to operate differently from any other character. He is never too bothered by his celebrity persona, only briefly taking a break from it to go incognito and not exploring why he wanted to escape it.

The book ends with the Celebrity as he was before, delighted to have returned to fame, making celebrity seem like a flaw in his personality that drives him to seek and find endless validation instead of comprehending a system with tremendous influence over him that he has little control over. Churchill's novel, as an indicator of the attitudes of his historical period, shows a widespread presence of animosity toward celebrities, with the success of his book relying on people who enjoy seeing a pompous celebrity be characterized as a fool. But it also implies that celebrity worship was likewise widespread; otherwise the book would not be as relevant as it was, meaning that there existed a large culture that lionized figures and loyally delighted over them.

The Celebrity gives us insight into the culture of the earliest twentieth century and was remarkably before its time in its depiction of the narcissism of a modern celebrity. One wonders if it was on Jay Gatsby's bookshelf.

A similar insight into the soul-destroying power of modern celebrity arrived in 1955 with Al Morgan's bestselling but now forgotten novel, *The Great Man*.[7] It is the story of Herb Fuller, a beloved radio and TV host who ingratiates himself with millions of viewers with his folksy charm and warmth. The resemblances to Arthur Godfrey are not coincidental. When Fuller dies in a car crash, the shocked nation goes into mourning.

A young reporter, Ed Harris, is given a week to prepare a TV tribute to the broadcaster. What he discovers is "the big lie." Fuller is in fact an opportunist, cheater, lecher, and drunkard. The newspapers have conspired in this public artifice to keep the great man great "for upon the greatness hang the meal tickets of thousands." His sincerity and friendliness are "used to sell cigarettes and soap." (The actor Jose Ferrer later directed and starred in the 1956 movie version of *The Great Man*.) The inescapable message is that, in the earliest days of television, there was already widespread concern about the selling of celebrity.

Today, celebrities tell their stories in memoirs as a duty forced on them by their agents and their fans. They can publish them to supplement a thriving career or to give a declining career a boost with the allure of finally-let-it-all-hang-out details. Sometimes a memoir launches a career all on its own, as in the case of Frank McCourt's *Angela's Ashes*. Regardless of its purpose, however, every celebrity memoir is an attempt at creating, packaging, and selling a personal myth.

One of the first was the actress Sarah Bernhardt with her memoir, *My Double Life*, which proclaimed her nonconformist lifestyle and personal defiance. According to Sharon Marcus, Bernhardt became "the godmother of modern celebrity" because she "invented many of the features of celebrity culture that remain in place to this day. She was one of the first figures to use modern media to achieve truly global celebrity by courting controversy, imitation, and evaluation, as well as one of the first to affect crowds so strongly that many journalists found her supporters alarming."[8]

In keeping with his flamboyant business model, the impresario P. T. Barnum likewise "wrote a controversial autobiography" filled with hokum to which "the backlash . . . was severe, and readers felt betrayed and swindled."[9]

While it was clear that the memoir could be another way celebrities could capitalize on their fame, the confessional narrative of overcoming challenges most celebrities use today had not yet been refined. Charles Lindbergh, for example, wrote a "dutiful" early memoir that made no effort to dress up his matter-of-fact writing.[10] It was well-received but nowhere near as successful as the phenomenally popular *Of Flight and Life*, written twenty years later in 1948.[11] This book was not a memoir as such, but as Brian Horrigan writes, it finds Lindbergh in high autobiographical mode and has a "stunning" spirituality uncommon to most celebrity books.[12]

Lindbergh was one of only a few celebrities to write more than one memoir. The formation of today's structured celebrity memoir began with the numerous attempts and styles found in Lindbergh's comparatively vast oeuvre. In 1953, he published *The Spirit of St. Louis*, what Brian Horrigan calls a "classic American epic" made of both "narrative" and "passages of evocative memoir."[13] *The Spirit of St. Louis* won a Pulitzer Prize, establishing it not only as the leader of a new frontier in celebrity memoir but also as a work of literary merit. There was also the posthumous *Autobiography of Values*, a collection of Lindbergh's memories and reflections written toward the end of his life. In none of these books, of course, did Lindbergh mention the secret of his multiple wives and families hidden across Europe. In that sense, he fulfilled the foreboding of celebrity-as-hypocrite made by Winston Churchill in *The Celebrity*.

Other early celebrities failed to capitalize on the opportunity of the memoir—or managed to do so only after their deaths. Thomas Edison, the celebrity inventor who once endeavored to record Sarah Bernhardt, would often "pretend that nothing had changed, that he was indifferent as ever" to his newfound celebrity.[14] Perhaps this is one reason he never published a memoir of his own, despite his "hunger for credit" in most things.[15] The myth created by his own companies may have been enough to sustain his legacy.

Other early celebrities, like Marilyn Monroe, wrote memoirs that were published posthumously. *My Story*, written at the height of her fame but not published until more than a decade after her death, deals in the narrative of overcoming challenges we have come to know in celebrity memoirs. The memoir describes the ups and downs of Monroe's early life and career—and its posthumous publication lends it an air of reclamation, putting her personal myth in her own words even after her death.[16]

In *Blonde*, her richly allusive novel about Monroe, Joyce Carol Oates delves deeper into the themes that shadowed Monroe's life as a celebrity—the rapes, molestations, miscarriages, abortions, predatory males, and voracious fans. Here we have the blind power of mythmaking in Hollywood, seen through the lens of one life. In that sense, it is the opposite of *The Celebrity*—the fault is not in the stars but in the people who create and enable them. "As Oates watched all of Monroe's movies," writes Elaine Showalter, "[and] learned more about her intelligence and humor, her determination to be seen as a serious actress, and the intersection of her career with multiple strands of mid-twentieth-century American culture—sports, religion, crime, theatre, politics—she realized that she needed a larger fictional form to explore a woman who was much more than a victim."[17]

Many modern celebrity memoir writers shape their myths by the traumas they've overcome. Sometimes they are self-inflicted, sometimes not. In her 2022 memoir, *Out of the Corner*, the actress Jennifer Grey details her struggles with cocaine, sex, and plastic surgery. Likewise, Selma Blair in *Mean Baby* discusses her alcoholism, sexual assaults, two suicide attempts, and eventual recovery.

In his memoir *Brat*, actor and director Andrew McCarthy writes candidly about his alcoholism:

> One of the predominant aspects of alcohol abuse is the baffling power it exerts over its victims. While someone else might have heeded this early warning sign of potential trouble on the horizon, I ignored the implications and instead focused on the more immediate problem of damage control.[18]

Here, McCarthy places the blame on himself for dismissing the signs of alcohol abuse. He is the one who eventually redeems himself, checking himself into the hospital after "[sobbing] at the disorder and chaos that my life had become."[19] Although he acknowledges his helplessness in the situation (note that in the passage above he is a "victim" of alcoholism, not its enabler), he also takes responsibility for the resolution of his largest personal issue.

Where McCarthy frames himself as both the cause and remedy of his trauma, other celebrities frame their lives around external incidents from which they restore their lives. In his account of his experiences on ABC's *The Bachelor*, contestant Matt James tells how he felt exploited by the series in the aftermath of the Black Lives Matter movement. "In my conversion from person to prop, key pieces of me were left behind," James said later, explaining why the series turned him into "a sideshow."[20]

In *Going There*, journalist Katie Couric writes of one personal and one professional incident from which she had to fight her way back. The first, more personal incident was the death of her husband, Jay, from colorectal cancer.[21] The chapters that follow her description of this tragedy primarily focus on her grief and recovery. Although Jay comes up in the memoir several times after his death, the second part of the book closes with a friend driving Couric and her family "back to our lives," implying a sense of moving forward.[22]

The professional obstacles faced by Couric were many, but one seemed particularly difficult to overcome—the failure of her run as an anchor on *CBS Evening News* and host on *60 Minutes*.[23] Couric cites not only the frequent criticism her anchoring drew but also her own regret at certain interviewing choices: "If I could have just one do-over, this would be it," she writes in regard to an interview with Elizabeth Edwards.[24] Chapter names like "She's Toast" and "The Fall of Rome" further emphasize how detrimental Couric's time at CBS was for her career—in short, she "was drowning."[25] There were other professional setbacks, such as the sexual harassment allegations against her professional partner Matt Lauer, but none seemed so personally disheartening as Couric's poor reception on CBS.[26] The book ends, however, with Couric taking out "a new lease on my professional life."[27]

Interestingly, on the first page of his memoir published the year before the notorious slap at the Oscars, Will Smith had all but predicted the incident as resulting from his lifelong fear of "being seen as weak." As a nine-year-old, he had failed to stand up for his mother when his father struck her. "Will Smith is largely a construction," he wrote, "a carefully crafted and honed character designed to protect himself. To hide myself from the world. To hide the coward."[28] He continues, "It's amazing how skewed your vision can become when you see the present through the lens of your past," referring to his constant awareness and expectation of violence as a result of his upbringing.[29] While this particular trauma was external, Smith also describes the internal challenges he faced. At one point, he writes, "I was *worse* than broke—I was in the *hole*. The walls were tumbling down. I had enjoyed Sodom and Gomorrah way more than I was enjoying Jericho."[30] He demonstrates a recognition of his situation and takes responsibility, saying, "I didn't pay my taxes," rather than blaming his situation on anyone else.[31] Like Couric, his book goes challenge by challenge until it leads to a hopeful embrace of love and bravery, which Smith describes as "learning to continue forward even when you're terrified."[32]

What all three memoirs have in common, besides their challenge/reward structure, is the construction of a personal myth. Smith puts this most explicitly:

> We tend to think of our personalities as fixed and solid. We think of our likes and dislikes, our beliefs, our nationalities, our political affiliations and religious convictions, our mannerisms, our sexual predilections, et cetera, as *set*, as *us*. But the reality is, most of the things that we think of as *us* are *learned* habits and patterns, and entirely malleable, and the danger when actors venture out to the far ends of our consciousness is that sometimes we lose the bread crumbs marking out way home. We realize that the characters we play in a film are no different than the characters we play in life. Will Smith is no more "real" than Paul [the dissembling character he plays in the 1993 movie *Six Degrees of Separation*]— they're both characters that were invented, practiced, and performed, reinforced, and refined by friends, loved ones, and the external world. What you think of as your "self" is a fragile construct.[33]

This is Smith's own definition of what McAdams might call the personal myth, or history of the self. If what Smith writes is true—that the self is a construct—it reinforces the idea that each celebrity is manufacturing their own personal myth, or projection of the self, in their memoir. This allows them to utilize a narrative structure that feels more like a story than an actual life. Each challenge is overcome in an episodic fashion, and the memoir often ends with a triumphant, hopeful witticism about how the author will continue to overcome the rest of life's challenges. Creating a personal myth allows celebrities to create just that—a myth, woven specifically to highlight their defeats, their resilience, their comebacks, and their path forward.

Movie biographies are another way to capture celebrity. Unlike the memoir, biopics approach a person from an outside perspective, conveying a director's vision rather than a personal one. It seems that there are seven semi-distinct categories of people who have their lives dramatized:

- Historical figures, like Abraham Lincoln and Harriet Tubman
- Criminals, like Frank Abagnale Jr. and Bonnie and Clyde
- Heroes, like Chesley Sullenberger in *Sully* and Chris Kyle in *American Sniper*
- People made famous by their profession or genius, like Stephen Hawking and Mark Zuckerberg
- Politicians, royals, and activists—such as Dick Cheney, Malcolm X, Princess Diana, Mahatma Gandhi, and Harvey Milk
- Athletes, like Muhammad Ali and Tonya Harding
- Entertainers—primarily but not exclusively limited to actors and musicians

Celebrities make up a large portion of the list. Often, the privilege of having a biopic made about oneself speaks to celebrity status, regardless of whether or not one is considered a celebrity in the Hollywood sense (that is, an actor or singer, or someone in "the industry"). There is, however, a fine line between a celebrity who receives the biopic treatment and a biopic about someone who is simply famous. Some biopics walk the line between both—was Stephen Hawking a celebrity scientist or a scientist who was famous for his work? A critic at *The Guardian* complains that the Hawking biopic, *The Theory of Everything*, focuses on the "emotional punch" of Hawking's struggle with ALS, rather than his "academic acclaim."[34] The film is more interested in the person than what made him famous—but regardless, the biopic exists only because Hawking was a notable person. Such is the paradox of the sympathetic biopic.

It seems that most modern biopics approach their subjects with a sympathetic view. This is especially true with female celebrities. The 2021 documentary *Framing Britney Spears* is one of the most recent films to highlight what Sara Lampert, writing in the *Washington Post*, calls "the limits of women's celebrity power . . . to navigate an industry that infantilizes them while subjecting them to narrow, and often contradictory, gendered standards."[35]

In her review of *Judy*, a biopic starring Renée Zellweger as Judy Garland, Manohla Dargis of the *New York Times* calls this narrative the "oft-told tragedy of greatness devoured by fame, by the entertainment machine, the audience's habit-forming adoration and bad personal choices."[36] *Judy* examines the end of the actress's life, painting her as "broke, substance-addled, and all but unemployable." Like many biopics, *Judy* is about the pitfalls of celebrity.[37] It takes shots at the very industry it is a part of, noting both the power and prison that fame gave Garland. Over the course of the film, Garland must take advantage of her fame in London to make enough money to remedy the consequences of her celebrity. It is celebrity that makes her and celebrity that destroys her—at least according to Hollywood. Garland herself first explored this route in *A Star Is Born*, the 1954 movie built on the idea that if a woman becomes a celebrity, or more successful than her man, she loses him.

I, Tonya, a biopic about figure skater Tonya Harding, also approaches its subject "with unexpected sympathy."[38] On Roger Ebert.com, the critic praises the film for being "affectionately mocking . . . without mocking Harding herself," showing "great kindness and emotional charity for this wounded figure."[39] Celebrity is less a destructive force for Harding than an ideal she is expected to chase. Nancy Kerrigan, her rival in reality and movie, embodies the "froufrou femininity" that the world expects of Harding—instead, journalists "called her 'white trash' and 'old Thunder Thighs.'"[40] The film acknowledges this mistreatment, pausing to "lecture the audience on its complicity in how [Harding] was treated" for the duration of her fame. However, some critics argue that creating a sympathetic narrative for Harding turns her into a one-dimensional figure, "a character in a drama, reduced to her function of her own story."[41] This is the nature of all biopics. By viewing their subjects from a distance, they diverge from the personal myth of the memoir and create a myth of artistic perception.

Biopics typically take a negative view of the experience of celebrity, observing either how their subjects fall victim to its effects (like Harding and Garland) or how they conquer it. Pablo Larraín's biopic about Jackie Kennedy Onassis is an example of the latter, exploring "the transformation of lived experience into myth."[42] Doing so brings with it the typically dehumanizing negative effects of celebrity. Howard University professor Oline Eaton writes of Onassis:

> The dismissal of the "real person" in such analysis ignores the tensions arising when we, in Susan Sontag's words, turn "people into objects that can be symbolically possessed." This is not to suggest that we do not use celebrities as objects or signs in our daily lives, for we often do. As Adam Gopnik wrote in the *New Yorker* upon the death of Jacqueline Kennedy Onassis, "Everything that we Americans did to her tried to turn her into an object . . . and everything she did was to try to make herself back into a subject." These tensions between a cultural imagining of the individual and the individual's sense of herself and her life are worth exploring."[43]

Eaton's and Gopnik's analyses poke at what makes celebrity so excruciating, particularly for women. Like Marilyn Monroe, Onassis was constantly forced to defend herself against the consequences of her celebrity. She testified that paparazzo

Ron Galella "made her life 'intolerable, almost unlivable,' and that she had 'no peace, no peace of mind.' "[44] Larraín frames the movie around an interview Onassis gave one week after John F. Kennedy's death. Like *I, Tonya*, *Jackie* turns its subject from person to stereotype in order to portray her sympathetically. In the words of Manohla Dargis in the *New York Times*, "she was the Widow—an embodiment of grief, symbol of strength, tower of dignity and, crucially, architect of brilliant political theater."[45] By turning her into an archetype, the movie also "takes her personhood for granted."[46] This is a necessary effect of the redemption narrative, through which Larraín "observes the exhausted, conflicted Jackie as she attempts to disentangle her own perspective, her own legacy, and, perhaps hardest of all, her own grief from a tragedy shared by millions."[47]

These consequences often went unnoticed in their time, and many biopics attempt to bring attention to injustices past and redeem their subjects. *Pam & Tommy*, a 2022 miniseries about Pamela (*Baywatch*) Anderson's leaked sex tape, criticizes the objectification Anderson faced in comparison to her partner Tommy Lee (the drummer of Mötley Crüe). The *Washington Post*'s Inkoo Kang called the series "the most layered and sympathetic treatment Pamela Anderson has ever gotten from the media."[48] Shirley Li of *The Atlantic* said that the show is "telling the feminist branch of the story."[49] *Pam & Tommy* engages in the redemption narrative, attempting to give Anderson a voice and reveal how she was victimized by the urge to objectify celebrities, particularly women. However, it also makes the same mistake as most biopics—it objectifies Anderson in trying to redeem her. Anderson herself "wasn't interested" in being involved in the series and never gave permission for it to tell her story. [50] Adding depth and humanity to the character fell to the actress portraying her, Lily James, who "finds subtleties in a woman that Hollywood and the media want to make into a sex cartoon."[51] Otherwise, she remains a storytelling device in a sharp criticism of the media's "high-tech slut shaming."[52] As with the other films, *Pam & Tommy* observes the various negative effects on women as a result of celebrity, giving Anderson the sympathy she lacked during the scandal itself.

Both memoirs and movie biographies have similar goals: to create sympathy, to redeem, to give a more personal perspective of a life lived in the public eye. They differ in their execution. The memoir purports to be an intimate, personal story told by the protagonist herself. The biopic approaches the subject with an inherently external view, sometimes with no personal input from the protagonist themselves. However, both maintain a degree of artificiality in constructing their narratives. The stories they tell may not be accurate, but they may be necessary. In her memoir, Selma Blair speaks for her caste when she rightly quotes Joan Didion from *The White Album:* "We tell ourselves stories in order to live."[53]

CHAPTER 12

SHAPE-SHIFTING

Cameos and Podcasts

Have a happy birthday!" hollers a recognizable voice from the screen on your smartphone. No, it's not a family member on FaceTime or a close friend's Instagram Story. It's the comedian Gilbert Gottfried, sitting in his bathroom, recording a greeting to a fan on the app called Cameo. Before he died in April 2022, Gottfried had recorded twelve thousand personalized messages for his fans and families, which, at $175 a clip, earned him over $2 million.[1]

In the twenty-first century, new technologies are once again transforming the world of celebrity. Cameo, which was founded in 2017, sells five thousand videos a day, all recorded by the forty thousand "celebrity talents" on their roster, ranging from retired athletes (Misty May-Treanor) and TV stars (Larry Thomas, the "Soup Nazi" on *Seinfeld*) to rappers (Snoop Dogg).

The videos are primarily commissioned as surprise gifts, most often for birthdays and holidays, but requests can get creative: marriage proposals, pep talks, and wisecracks. ("Can you tell my brother to give up on golf?") And of course, celebrities are often asked to reproduce iconic catchphrases, like *Succession* star Brian Cox, who signs off many messages with a hearty, "Fuck off!"[2] Even when messages are full of profanity, reactions are widely positive, with fans often submitting emotional reaction videos and leaving five-star ratings. (Yes, that's right, you can now leave a review for Golden Globe–winning actors.)

What gets lost in the transaction is the mystique we used to grant to celebrities. We can't imagine Elizabeth Taylor throwing digital kisses from her bathroom. Steven Galanis, Cameo's co-founder and CEO, describes the app as an emblem of a digital world without so many barriers between stars and their fans.[3] "I think that in a world where people are more famous than ever before, we're going to need to lean on technology to have that human interaction," says Galanis, a former trader and LinkedIn employee.[4] So much for the days when avid fans skimmed through *People* at a newsstand.

As with Instagram or other crowdfunded platforms, like OnlyFans, stars are no longer "kept behind lock and key of management and media."[5] Celebrities who qualify as "talent" on Cameo need "at least 25,000 followers on Instagram or [to] be notable in some other way."[6] They get to set their own prices, choose which requests to accept, and record the video from their smartphone, all in the span of a few minutes. Paradoxically, the low production value of these clips can often be more endearing to fans than a high-res film because it confirms a sense of authenticity. "The more natural I am, the better, because with people that's their connection" reports sports personality Ozzie Guillén.[7]

Galanis uses the analogy of running into someone famous in a restaurant: "You're going to tell everybody for the next 20 years like, wow, I met XYZ. They were a great person. Likewise, if you go up to somebody famous, and they blow you off, you're going to tell everyone that they're terrible."[8] Cameo creates a virtual space for the former, clarifying the transaction so that fans can have a memorable experience and celebrities can make sure they are building positive relationships with their supporters.

In return, Cameo takes a 25 percent cut of the sale.[9] The concept was born, of all places, at the funeral of Galanis's grandmother when a friend showed Galanis a personalized message NFL player Cassius Marsh had recorded congratulating a fan on the birth of his son. The fan had such an ecstatic reaction to the clip that Galanis concluded, " 'This is the new autograph.' "[10]

During the coronavirus pandemic, as the world spun into lockdowns, fans and celebrities alike were reliant on the internet for connection. Cameo ballooned to over three hundred employees and earned the status of a "unicorn" (a privately owned startup valued at over $1 billion), growing at a rate that shocked even fellow unicorn entrepreneurs. [11]

Brushing aside initial criticism of the platform—"it's a platform for washed-up celebs to cash in on nostalgia"—Galanis portrays Cameo as a social media network with the ability to make a real difference in the lives of beloved personalities.[12] When asked by *New York Times* reporter Kara Swisher whether Cameo promotes the idea that "everybody is for sale and that people have a price," Galanis didn't disagree but rushed to respond, "That's always been true." Galanis acknowledges that celebrities have always been part of a business model that cashes in on their influence, but these practices "weren't working for all but maybe the very, very top of the heap. And . . . that gap between fame and monetization continues to widen."[13]

As a sports enthusiast, Galanis was crushed to find out how infrequently fame correlates to financial stability for some of the industry's greatest players. "In sports, the top 2% of athletes make 99% of all the revenue," he said. "In music, the top 1% of artists make over 90% of the concert revenue, etc. For a lot of people, direct-to-fan income streams like Cameo are the only thing that's keeping them afloat."[14]

Now Dan Bernstein, a sports news anchor, can record a few videos for fans from a supermarket parking lot before heading inside to buy groceries.[15] On a larger scale, Brian Baumgartner, the actor who played Kevin in the TV series *The Office*, was Cameo's highest earner in 2020, making over $1 million.[16]

And, while comedians might be the most popular creators, other familiar faces have accounts, including Republican politician Sarah Palin, who reported earning $211,529 on Cameo in 2021, thousands more than she would make as a member of Congress.[17]

Stars have also adopted the app as a way to fundraise for charitable causes: Sarah Jessica Parker raked in tens of thousands in just a few days for the New York City Ballet before their fall fashion gala, and Alex Borstein created an account to raise money for mothers in Ukraine. As she told her 230,000 Instagram followers, "I can cuss at you, I can say filthy things, if you want, and we're helping moms and kids. Isn't that nice?"[18]

Due to the personal style of Cameo's content, gaining fan and celebrity trust was an essential first step for the startup. In the early days of Cameo, Galanis was at the forefront of recruiting talent, often traveling cross-country to sit down with stars one-on-one and pitch them his vision. It was this founding principle that saved the organization when it faced their first scandal. Galanis describes the event as their personal Armageddon—an event that threatened to destroy the hard-earned trust between Cameo and its celebrity creators. In November 2018, NFL quarterback Brett Favre, comedian Andy Dick, and rapper Soulja Boy were each commissioned by a white supremacist group to record messages they thought were supporting American military troops, but they unknowingly repeated coded anti-Semitic rhetoric. Galanis instructed his staff to comfort each celebrity individually and got to work reporting all the copies of the video that had been dispersed across social media as hate speech.[19] However, he got no response from these platforms until he realized he could report them as a copyright violation on behalf of the creators. Only then did videos start to get taken down.[20]

Cameo is certainly thinking about finding new ways to engage with users' wallets following a drop in engagement as pandemic restrictions are lifted. Galanis is certain the desire for a personal connection between celebrities and their fans will never run dry. Even as the format for these relationships changes, a birthday wish from a star will always sound sweet.

Another technology that has quietly flourished in the twenty-first century and given celebrities a bright new way to access their fans is podcasting. Podcasts are booming, and, as with Cameo, the coronavirus pandemic is behind the surge. Millions of people all around the world are staying home and listening to podcasts on a daily basis.

A podcast is basically an on-demand talk radio show that combines the talk show format with the low-entry barrier of streaming services. Fans love the accessibility that podcasts provide to their favorite celebrities. Ardent listeners will be quick to tell you about the latest episode they heard and where they were when it happened: "I love listening to Conan O'Brien on my commute," or, "I caught up with Kate Hudson while on a run." Not only are podcasts an approachable way to consume content because of their hands-free, just-press-play format, but they also create a sense of closeness with their hosts. The sensation of having a celebrity rambling directly into your earbuds, "ums" and all, can be an extremely intimate experience. Just like Cameos and Instagram, podcasts feed into the authenticity market in which quantity of content is favored over artistic quality.

There are still big players like Barack and Michelle Obama, who in 2022 signed their production company, Higher Ground, to make podcasts and other audio programs with Amazon's Audible service. These biggest podcasts attract millions of listeners per episode.

One top-ten list compiled in February 2022 by the *All Top Everything* newsletter yielded an eclectic result, ranging from *The Joe Rogan Experience* to *True Crime*.[21]

1. THE JOE ROGAN EXPERIENCE
   Hosted by Joe Rogan
2. CRIME JUNKIE
   Hosted by Ashley Flowers and Brit Prawat
3. CALL HER DADDY
   Hosted by Alex Cooper
4. MY FAVORITE MURDER
   Hosted by Karen Kilgariff and Georgia Hardstark
5. THE BEN SHAPIRO SHOW
   Hosted by Ben Shapiro
6. THE DAILY
   Hosted by Michael Barbaro and Sabrina Tavernise
7. OFFICE LADIES
   Hosted by Angela Kinsey and Jenna Fischer
8. POD SAVE AMERICA
   Hosted by Jon Favreau, Jon Lovett, and Tommy Vietor
9. STUFF YOU SHOULD KNOW
   Hosted by Charles Bryant and Josh Clark
10. MORBID: A TRUE CRIME PODCAST
    Hosted by Ashleigh Kelley and Alaina Urquart

On this list, the most freshly coined celebrity is Alex Cooper, the twenty-seven-year-old host and producer of *Call Her Daddy*, the sex and dating show followed by millions and recently bought by Spotify for more than $60 million.[22] According to Julie Miller, writing in *Vanity Fair*, "One insider estimates that many celebrities could get a six-figure guarantee per year, with the biggest actors receiving between $1 million and $3 million to launch an unscripted podcast."[23] Scripted podcasts "offer less up-front money," but pose significant potential for future bonuses as they "can be adapted into TV shows, films, books, and so on."

The autonomy guaranteed by podcasts also attracts many celebrities. Robert Herting, a former agent at CAA, thinks that what appeals to A-list talent about podcasts is that "they can own it. They can control it. They can partner in it. They can be involved with the distribution decisions."

Many celebrities, such as Jamie Lee Curtis, feel that podcasts offer an "intimacy between host and listener" that draws them in. Rather than trying to sell something as talk show hosts often do, podcasts offer "a more authentic opportunity" to talk about other things like "friendship, not selling." Another advantage to podcasting is that it's less competitive than acting and thus may be easier for certain celebrities to foray into.

Entertainment Weekly notes that "celebrity podcasts are everywhere—and the deluge of downloads has only just begun." Why? Because on podcasts, "fans get a chance to really interact with the celebrities, and the celebrities get a chance to talk to their fan base about things they wouldn't talk about before."[24]

There are several more reasons why celebrities go into podcasting outlined in *Backtracks*, which acts as something of a trade publication for the podcasting industry. Podcasting can elevate a "mid-tier celebrity's brand," and more famous celebrities can use podcasts to simply "enhance" their following online.[25] Celebrities can even use podcasting as a way to "refine" or change their personal brand, or as a platform to talk about things they otherwise would not have a chance to.[26]

This can be a welcoming environment for the little guys. You don't need a big broadcast studio or to work for a radio station; you just need a mic and computer. One self-made entrepreneur is the journalist Kinsey Schofield, whose podcast *To Di For Daily* covers Princess Diana and her children and is distributed by Spotify. All told, she has an audience of 250,000, which she monetarizes through sponsorships, endorsements, and YouTube ads. As she puts it, happily, "I'm just flying by the seat of my pants."

Since the pandemic, podcasting has tipped from a medium for audio journalism into a playground for celebrities. No longer an uncharted territory, the podcast industry, now valued at

$1 billion, has mastered doling out enticing snippets of celebrity wisdom and anecdotes. The content resembles the formulaic tradition of celebrity memoirs: a balance of inspiring and re- latable stories that provides an uplifting look behind the scenes of their life. With episodes released every week, suddenly Rob Lowe can *really* become a part of your Sunday trips to Whole Foods and Katherine Ryan will become an essential companion to doing laundry.

This has particular significance for advertising, with an av- erage of 3.3 ads featured in each episode. Hosts often record ads themselves to contribute to a more seamless sound. This also lends endorsements a particular sense of authenticity when stars guarantee that they "actually use it *all* the time." A survey of "super listeners" in December 2020 found that 48 percent "said they pay more attention to advertising on podcasts than with other media."[27] The demographics of podcasts are exciting for advertisers: they're young (with a median age of thirty-four) and educated.[28] Clearly, podcasting is drawing attention as a new way for advertisers to reach a highly sought-after audience.

The rise of Spotify has further contributed to a celeb- rity-friendly ecosystem. For context, Spotify "feels like free" to users since they can simply make an account, download the application, and have access to millions of songs for free, although they can upgrade to a premium version without ads for a monthly subscription. To listen to a podcast on Spotify, one simply needs to look up "podcast" in the search bar and millions of different podcasts will appear.[29] Spotify has even cu- rated playlists of podcasts tailored for different moods and top- ics like "Top Podcasts of 2021" and "Daily Podcasts."[30] The sure indication of the reach and value of the podcast genre is that Spotify is paying Rogan $200 million for exclusive streaming rights through 2023.[31]

Professional athletes have been getting on the podcasting bandwagon, with mixed results. To hear an NBA player sitting in a hotel room talking about the game he just played or a tennis

player explaining why she lost her last match can be demysti-
fying. The mystique somehow vanishes with overexposure. As
Jeremy Gordon wrote about his experience listening to athletes
talking:

> The demystification process can, at times, be *too* thorough.
> I, and many others, watch sports in large part to be awed:
> Sometimes it seems truly unbelievable that someone like
> Steph Curry can do what he does, and the experience of wit-
> nessing it in real time, the act of creation right in front of
> you, provides inexplicable joy. Surprisingly, though, it turns
> out to be deeply enervating to hear these athletes talk about
> it. Sports, for them, is mostly a fun job they have, or used to
> have; they tend to have thoughts about every aspect of it be-
> sides the magic of the game itself.[32]

In sum, the newest digital means of accessing celebrities—
cameos and podcasts—are clearly intertwined. Many celebrities
have entered the podcasting world for reasons ranging from
furthering their personal brand to having more creative freedom and sometimes even rehabbing their careers. More and
more celebrities will be creating podcasts in the next few years.
The question before us now, as we will see in the next chapter, is
whether we need celebrities in the flesh at all.

CHAPTER 13

"R U REAL?"

There is a new It Girl in town. She pouts. She graces magazine covers, drops into haute couture fashion shows, and promotes luxury brands. In other words, she's everything we've come to expect from a Gen Z celebrity influencer. So much so that she just turned nineteen for the seventh time.

Miquela Sousa, or @LilMiquela, as her handle is known to her over three million Instagram followers, is a virtual influencer—also known as a CGI, or computer-generated image—who is a model, singer, and activist. Joining Instagram in April 2016, this self-described "19-year-old Robot living in LA" is an ersatz public personality, an artificial avatar who does not actually exist yet can speak to millions of fans from her digital platforms.

Initially the first of her kind, Miquela now represents a whole subcategory of social media culture as her cohort of peers has grown.[1] A pioneer in the emerging CGI influencer market, which has a projected value of $85 billion by 2028, Miquela has built her fame out of precisely targeted branding.[2] According to Aleks Eror, in an exposé about Miquela for *Highsnobiety*, the daily news, fashion, and design website, her attitude of fame for fame's sake signals a twenty-first-century phenomenon.[3] Using

Guy Debord's theory of celebrity proposed in *The Society of the Spectacle*, Eror explains that twentieth-century stars (think athletes, actresses, even famous minds) cultivated a relatable public persona to commercialize their success, but this was always secondary to their initial talent.

As Miquela pushes "Doing it for the 'gram" to the max—that is, calculating her every act for its appeal on Instagram—she becomes a case study for the future of celebrity culture in a digital age. Through understanding the feedback she gets from the choices involved in building this character, we can begin to answer the emerging questions:

What are the values that evoke empathy and inspire loyalty among young generations? How has transparent inauthenticity paradoxically led to trust, and what are its limits? And what comes next if corporate brands no longer need a human to connect with consumers?

Lil Miquela's Instagram presence resembles the accounts of countless other influencers—she promotes her music, collaborates with luxury brands (including Prada and Supreme), and posts candid selfies with her friends and love interests (a mix of other robots and human celebrities)—but none of it is real.[4] Or, rather, none of it is reality. The music she produces can really be streamed by her almost two hundred thousand monthly listeners on Spotify. The donation links for Black Lives Matter funds she shares connect to legitimate nonprofits. And the money she rakes in through product promotion is most definitely out there (an estimated $12,000 to $25,000 per sponsored post).[5]

But to whom is it really going?

The Svengali behind Miquela is the Los Angeles–based media studio group Brud, most recently valued at $125 million.[6] While it may portray itself as a tech startup, those closer to the operation have described it as "performance art" supported by a team of media experts rather than coders.[7] In a rare interview on Reid Hoffman's podcast, *Masters of Scale*, Brud cofounder and Miquela's creator Trevor McFedries laid out his motivation for starting the company: to build "a bridge to empathy." He sees virtual influencers as powerful agents for branding and activism on par with Marvel characters.[8] McFedries was inspired by the ability of these heroes to connect with a wide range of audiences, despite being fictional superhumans, and he picked social media as the modern-day equivalent to weekly comic books. He hopes that promoting a nonhuman voice to the level of celebrity could help remove the burden of fame from one set of shoulders, thus avoiding the burnout or sacrifice of privacy endemic to the role for humans.[9]

Critics have pointed out that removing the human spokesperson also removes the chance of disagreement between the seller and the influencer.[10] Could users connect to a message that wasn't endorsed by a real human? In many ways, this question about authenticity also pertains to human influencers, because users have begun to doubt any message attached to sponsored content. A 2019 study found that very little separates the perceived authenticity of a virtual influencer like Miquela from the authenticity attributed to an actual human being.[11]

The study also found that 41 percent of respondents followed a virtual influencer without realizing the account actually belonged to a CGI. As McFedries predicted, the *human* component of online connection is taking a back seat to a convincing sense of honesty. More than any other influencer, Miquela truly does not exist outside of her celebrity status, so everything she does is an intentional contribution to her public image. Yet despite early skepticism, fans (affectionately referred to as Miqaliens) have embraced Miquela for her openness about being artificial.[12] In their academic study of CGI influencers, Elena Block and Rob Lovegrove coined the term "honest fakery" to describe this approach.[13] After seeing Miquela lurking across social media platforms (including on the accounts of Brud's two other characters, Blawko and Bermuda), Block and Lovegrove determined that Miquela stepped in at an opportune moment in a "post-trust world."

While other influencers work fiercely to leave an impression of authenticity on the internet, whether through posting #NoFilter selfies or appearing to have on-camera breakdowns, Miquela flies in the face of that tactic. Paradoxically, consumers seem to respect her choice. It's the reason that one young follower responded to an eleven-year-old's comment, "She's not real," with, "She's realer than Kylie Jenner."[14]

However, the honestly fake quality that Miquela fabricates isn't as transparent as it may seem. Those who try to learn more about her quickly hit a brick wall. All the reporting on this virtual celebrity, even supposedly direct interviews, is shrouded in mystery. At the root of all this smoke and mirrors is an uncertainty about Miquela's creation. Yes, she may frequently call herself a robot, but there are no indications that a physical robot exists. Similarly, those who have called her AI lack proof, leading multiple journalists to propose that Miquela is more likely the product of a team of writers and graphic designers. In their essay for the *Handbook of Research on Deception, Fake News, and Misinformation Online*, Raymond Blanton and Darlene Carbajal criticize Brud for promoting contradictory language about Miquela, referring to her as both technology and a conscious being, sometimes in the same sentence.[15] Combined with the hyperrealistic portrayal of Miquela's lifestyle—she even went into lockdown and worked from home during the pandemic—social media users coming across her in their feed might not recognize her virtual origins.

This creates several new fields of concern regarding celebrity power, particularly considering that a large portion of Miquela's audience are minors who may be particularly impressionable.[16] Not only must the Federal Trade Commission respond to the growing impact of virtual influencers, but also basic internet literacy needs to teach users how to parse the real from the fabricated. For example, Brud has received criticism for depicting Miquela with a shapely figure that is unrealistic for humans. An

Instagram post on Miquela's account in 2020 showed her posing with human model Lindsay Vrckovnik. It received the standard comments of disbelief and confusion—"Wait, r u a robot?"— but also comments comparing their bodies, including, "The robot more pretty."[17] Brud quickly realized their mistake, and thanks to the malleable nature of Miquela, altered her appearance going forward. This move—to quickly edit her appearance and appease her followers—speaks to the initial issue: even in their attempt to make Miquela more like her human followers, Brud emphasizes the abilities that set her apart.

Similarly, the blurred boundary between human and robot is integral to Miquela's strategy for building a strong parasocial relationship between herself and her fans. Like many influencers with such a large following, Miquela is not able to reach each one individually. When asked about how she builds an "authentic connection" with followers, she offers a response similar to many human influencers: "Every relationship is a two-way street, and the relationship between artist and fan isn't any different. So, I guess my fans are engaged because I'm engaged. I try to listen to their stories and really become part of their lives. They're really there for me when I need them . . . like they're the reassuring voices in my head when I feel like things are going left."[18]

Here Miquela takes up a vulnerable tone to portray that she is as equally invested in the lives of her fans as they are in hers. As with human influencers, this is inherently impossible because the power dynamic between influencer and influenced places the former on a pedestal from which they can reap monetary benefits and fame, but which is literally and figuratively out of reach for her followers. And obviously, they are far too numerous for even a robot to form individual relationships with each of them. But what particularly distinguishes Miquela is her insistence on adopting human language. She talks about the "voices in [her] head" even though she has no mind to host these voices. Similarly, at another moment in the interview, she discusses her personal journey as a celebrity and mentions "a few messy lows—some of them have been public," implying that she has a private life off social media.[19]

In mimicking a human influencer, Miquela becomes more relatable to her followers. However, she simultaneously offers them opportunities to engage with her that are only possible because she isn't human. Such opportunities include polls in which fans can vote on aspects of Miquela's lifestyle, such as what color dress she will wear or which memories she should "unlock" next.[20] Not to be forgotten is Miquela's endless energy. She is always available for her fans and can dedicate every hour to creating content at a pace that human celebrities simply can't keep up with. Miquela isn't just copying the tactics of human celebrities; she's beating them at their own game.

That is not to say that Lil Miquela's story is free of conflict. Her public life over the past six years has been punctuated by scandals that can be broken down into two categories: scripted and less intentional. The former—scripted challenges—are a part of McFedries's plan to build a modern Marvel character, beginning with a compelling origin story. Once fans had bought into Miquela's brand, signified by a spike in her followers in 2017, it appears Brud strategized to keep their attention with a little drama.[21] In April 2018, just before the two-year anniversary of Miquela's introduction to Instagram, her account came under attack. Suddenly, all her content disappeared and was replaced by selfies of @BermudaIsBae, another virtual influencer and Miquela's blonde, Trump-supporting foil. Just as her fans have, Bermuda took issue with Miquela's misleading self-representation as human and demanded she tell her audience "the truth."[22] Following a threatening countdown and drawn-out negotiation, Miquela regained control of her Instagram account and posted a screenshot that models itself on other heartfelt celebrity apologies. The text prefaces, "I'm sure you guys have noticed I'm a pretty private person," and, "My hands are literally shaking," before announcing, "I'm not a human being."[23]

However, the story doesn't end there. After her coming-out as a robot, Miquela shares that she and Bermuda were created by Cain Intelligence, an AI company with sinister intentions for the future of robotics. Instead, she was rescued by Brud but felt betrayed by their secrecy. Suddenly, Miquela is cast as the victim of her own deception, a young adult rebelling against her pseudo-adoptive parents and apologizing to her fan base of friends. Relatable, right? This post received over two hundred thousand likes—two times more than any of the surrounding content—and drew the attention of journalists who, once again, hit dead ends while trying to report on Miquela. Cain Intelligence doesn't exist, and Bermuda, it turns out, is also operated by Brud.[24] Following live coverage of the scandal, Emilia Petrarca at *The Cut* declared the whole story a publicity stunt—except, of course, for the confirmation that Miquela is a robot.[25] Even in moments of supposed truth-telling, Brud writers continue to interweave reality and fiction. The inclusion of human attributes, like shaky hands in the post about Miquela confessing to being a robot, demonstrates how difficult it can be for close readers, let alone passersby, to separate reality from Brud's fantasy.

Over the following month, Miquela's Instagram captions documented her feelings of self-doubt and mistrust, using vague language. Clearly aware of the paradoxical empathy she evokes, one post formatted as a meme complained about the weight of "Finding out ur a robot and ur family lied to you" (tagging Brud's Instagram account) with the caption, "Who can relate?"[26] More narrative-driven posts like these were padded with sponsored content and a plug for her latest magazine cover story. To protect herself from criticism, Miquela asserted that she has separated from Brud, becoming a "#freeagent."[27] Of course this is impossible, as she can't exist or create new content without Brud. Another post stands out for its maneuvering of the "truth." "I owe you guys more honesty," begins the caption below a picture of Miquela casually posed in a white tank top:

> In trying to realize my truth, I'm trying to learn my fiction . . .
>
> I'm not sure I can comfortably identify as a woman of color.
>
> "Brown" was a choice made by a corporation.
>
> "Woman" was an option on a computer screen.
>
> My identity was a choice Brud made in order to sell me to brands, to appear "woke."
>
> I will never forgive them. I don't know if I will ever forgive myself.[28]

Once again, Miquela isolates herself from Brud in language written by Brud's staff. She fosters empathy among her fans by aligning herself with their perspective and portraying Brud as the culprit. By confronting the issue of Miquela's race and gender before the press, Brud can control the narrative (unlike another virtual model, Shudu, who appears as a Black woman and came under fire around the same time when it was discovered that her creator was a white male artist).[29] In an article entitled "This Is Fucky: Simulated Influencers Are Turning Identity into a Form of Currency," Rosa Boshier agrees with Miquela: her racial ambiguity and female identity *are* used by Brud to commodify multiculturalism for a white audience. Boshier argues:

> As a simulated influencer with an ever-growing following and brands behind her, ready to pay for access to a relatable, oppressed queer young woman of color without having to actually work with queer women of color, Miquela espouses vague messages about equality while simultaneously commodifying social progress for capital gain.[30]

What's particularly interesting in each of these cases is the response of fans. The comments sections are filled with followers rushing to comfort Miquela: "I wish you were real so I could hug you right now!"[31] Thanks to this narrative that separates Miquela from Brud, she can apologize and absolve herself of any guilt. Brud has discovered a way to let a celebrity escape from both the frame and the blame; a virtual influencer can always fall back upon their artificial origins when they make a controversial choice.

The same strategy can be seen at play during the accidental scandals Miquela has landed herself in. These include a Calvin Klein advertisement accused of queerbaiting after Miquela shared a kiss with heterosexual model Bella Hadid and a vlog about Miquela's experience being sexually assaulted in a rideshare. The necessary question to ask was whether the men behind the creation of a fictional character are using her to exploit the real pain of women of color and women who suffer sexual abuse.

In its public apology, Calvin Klein stated that its intentions for the video were to explore "the blurred lines between reality and imagination," and Miquela described her assailant as aggressively asking, "Are you real?"[32] Musician Kehlani tweeted "@lilmiquela, you're playing with real stories . . . real trauma."[33]

Even in instances of acknowledged mistakes, Miquela benefits from an artificial ability to strike her mistakes from the record, then overwhelm the few articles that remain on the subject with fresh content. Afterwards, she never has to be wary of her past leaking into her public image. For example, Brud can be certain their proprietary character will never misspeak about the incident in the future since they dictate her voice.

In fact, Block and Lovegrove suggest these events might not be media mistakes so much as Brud "testing the limits of their character and her storytelling prowess. But also, and simultaneously, they are aimed at boosting controversy and headlines."[34]

They group Miquela's activism, particularly her support of the Black Lives Matter movement, with these controversial incidents, explaining how each is an example of Miquela disrupting expectations for influencers. However, Miquela has created these disruptions only after performing the role of an influencer so convincingly. In the case that headlines ever begin to seriously threaten her fame, the creators can retreat—taking down content and "blaming" Brud's poor decision-making, which of course is their own.

Subsequently, none of these incidents have been a huge detriment to Miquela's rise. Instead, each has tested the meaning of truth on the internet and prolonged public interest while being careful to remain socially desirable. All the while, Miquela has continued to participate in the influencer market she claims to disrupt. Not only has Miquela mastered a form of twenty-first-century celebrity built upon branding, but she also has proven that she can infinitely rebrand herself. As McFedries's initial vision unfolds, it's clear that Miquela can procure a "sense of empathy" in almost any scenario using her "honest fakery."[35]

Watching the subtle yet intentional shifts in her character and content over the past six years has been daunting. What remains clear is the power of celebrity status to continue to survive on its own. In the latest phenomenon, the so-called deep fakes, advertisers create digital doppelgangers of real celebrities ranging from Elon Musk to Tom Cruise and Leonardo DiCaprio to populate their ads, with or without permission. What comes next is a mystery to industry experts and Instagram followers alike. However, it's evident that Miquela's elusive story, along with those of other "robot" creations, will be at the center of it.

CHAPTER 14

THE FUTURE OF FAME

The much acclaimed, but perhaps less well known in the twenty-first century, novelist John Updike once wrote: "Celebrity is a mask that eats into your face. As soon as one is aware of being 'somebody,' to be watched and listened to with extra interest, input ceases, and the performer goes blind and deaf in his overanimation. One can either see or be seen."[1]

What is celebrity doing to us? Is it rotting us from the inside individually, as Updike would have it, or is there broader damage—is it eating not only into the face of our culture but into our collective core values and our well-being as well? Do we have a way of understanding and describing what the boldface names are doing to the face of our democracy? More important, do we know how to repair the damage and treasure our heroes again?

Critics and scholars have historically dismissed celebrities as providing entertaining sideshows, without merit, distracting us from the important work of setting priorities in our lives and for our country. At *People*, I learned something about the celebrity future from the celebrity past. In 1983, I assigned myself to do a year-end story about a nerdy software engineer in Seattle no one had heard of. He was a twenty-three-year-old named Bill Gates who had dropped out of Harvard and founded a company with the oddly hyphenated name of Micro-Soft. The company had attracted early investors, but Gates himself was not yet a celebrity. I would be meeting a kid with a future.

Over a seafood dinner on the banks of Lake Washington, Gates told me about his life. His parents were affluent, and they sent him to the private Lakeside School, where, in seventh grade, he and his friends began writing software programs to schedule the school's classes. He then learned the BASIC computing language and formed a venture with his friend Paul Allen called Traf-O-Data to analyze traffic patterns in town.

Everything changed after Gates read a cover story in the January 1975 issue of *Popular Electronics* about a build-it-yourself home computer called the Altair. Gates and Allen set about to write a BASIC interpreter for the Altair and went to work for the parent company, MITS, in Albuquerque. Soon, thanks to an introduction from his mom, IBM approached him to write an operating system for their first home computer, the PC. Micro-Soft was suddenly transformed from an obscure startup to the hottest and biggest software company in the world.

I saved my transcript of our interview. Rereading it now, I noticed the details. Gates's vocabulary was peppered with his boyish mannerisms—such as runaway prefixes like "super"— as in "super-cool" and "super-important." His programmers, he said, wrote "slick, tight code." His manner was breezy, but his colleagues told me that his management style was sophisticated and aggressive. He was intense (he did not own a TV) and driven (writing up to one hundred of what we then called "electronic letters" a day). "I'm still fairly hard-core," he told me about his work ethic.

What I was seeing was an early *image* of a Silicon Valley celebrity—the brilliant boy, the early success, already handled by a careful publicist. As Daniel Boorstin wrote in *The Image*, "Since the Graphic Revolution, the celebrity overshadows the hero by the same relentless law which gives other kinds of pseudo-events an overshadowing power. In the creation of a celebrity somebody always has an interest—[reporters] needing stories, press agents paid to make celebrities, and the celebrit[ies] [themselves]."[2]

If the idea of celebrity grows as its images are multiplied by new technologies, Microsoft (the hyphen soon disappeared) and other software companies did more than anyone to supply the images on our computers, in our hands, and in our brains that would create the armature of celebrity.

My interview with Gates ran in a *People* special issue called "The 25 Most Intriguing People of 1983." The other such Intriguers that year were a celebrity grab bag that included Michael Jackson, Joan Rivers, Mr. T, Eddie Murphy, Matthew Broderick, and Fidel Castro.

Much later, Gates had been through an entire celebrity life cycle. After becoming one of the world's wealthiest people, he and Warren Buffett initiated the Giving Pledge to encourage billionaires to leave half of their fortunes to philanthropic causes. By then he had achieved mega-celebrity status and fostered many good works—along with acquiring a divorce.

Gates was hardly the first alpha male to step into those choppy waters. The would-be president John Edwards put it well when he was interviewed by ABC's Bob Woodruff on *Nightline* in 2008 about the exposure of his extramarital affair two years earlier. Edwards did not mince his words:

Ego. Self-focus, self-importance. Now, I was slapped down to the ground when my son Wade died in 1996. But then after that I ran for the Senate and I got elected to the Senate and here we go again, it's the same old thing again. Adulation, respect, admiration. Then I went from being a senator, a young senator to being considered for vice president, running for president, being a vice presidential candidate and becoming a national public figure. All of which fed a self-focus, an egotism, a narcissism that leads you to believe that you can do whatever you want. You're invincible. And there will be no consequences. And nothing, nothing could be further from the truth.[3]

As the public careers of Bill Gates and John Edwards demonstrate, our human psyche likes to think of celebrities as its flawed gods. We don't want them all good or all bad. So Bill Gates in his philanthropic celebrity role can be seen as a boon to humankind. He has used his celebrity to advance important causes related to global issues involving health and other fundamental human needs. Yet he can also be seen as a fallen angel, just as Bill Cosby or Elizabeth Holmes of Theranos can. We like to see the full spectrum of behavior and values in the ephemeral deities we call celebrities.[4]

Today, if we look internationally, we see that the production and consumption of celebrity is the product of collaborations between the media and willing publics everywhere. This is especially true in South Asia, where self-styled armies of fans have created their own virtual economies. The Chinese are so aware of this that the government has intensified its digital crackdown on celebrities and social media on the grounds that the armies of fans create "chaos" and promote "extravagant pleasure." In 2021, the Cyberspace Administration of China released social media rules for celebrities. Those with fame won't be allowed to show off wealth. Celebrities are banned from publishing false or private information, provoking fans, and spreading rumors.[5]

In South Korea, the K-pop genre of powerful vocals, fashion-forward styles, and eye-popping choreography has created an international phenomenon. While many individual Western pop groups have obtained global fame—one immediately thinks of the British boy band One Direction or maybe even the Beatles—the global success of K-pop is the result of the sustained, decades-long industry-wide success of an entire genre. That is, K-pop—along with much of South Korean popular music since the late 1990s—has routinely been manufactured and marketed as an export commodity, drawing from and synthesizing previous music trends in East Asia, such as idol pop and dance pop.[6]

The success and longevity of many K-pop groups is often contingent on entertainment companies successfully building a media universe for fans to engage with. K-pop's most successful group act to date is BTS, or the Bangtan Boys, debuting in 2013. It is an all-boys band that has been nominated for two Grammys, a challenging feat for non-Western artists, and in 2021 alone the group had three number-one hits on *Billboard*. HYBE, BTS's management company, posts multiple videos nearly every day to the band's personal YouTube channel, BANGTANTV, which has more than seventy million subscribers.[7]

The messages of K-pop, more than those of Western artists, are often about self-confidence and empowerment. BTS's slogan for many years was "Love Yourself" (several of their albums were similarly titled). This content has attracted a self-styled army primarily made up of women.[8] The members of BTS have spoken at the United Nations and were invited to the White House in May 2022 to help the Biden administration commemorate Asian/Pacific American Heritage Month. What remains uncertain, though, is whether over time BTS will successfully spin off individual artists—its own Harry Styleses or Paul McCartneys.

The internet and social media have fostered countless celebrities and celebrity worshippers, at the expense of our civic life. But does the success of K-pop suggest that we should be looking more carefully at a contrarian point of view? Can the energies of celebrity culture offer a meaningful way to draw their fans into contributing to the positive work of making a more civil society? Can we build hope on the idea that celebrities will someday lead their fan communities toward social good?

This question was first taken on by the English scholars Nick Couldry and Tim Markham in their 2007 paper, "Celebrity Culture and Public Connection: Bridge or Chasm?"[9] They asked a selected and diverse group of diarists, split across gender and age categories between eighteen and sixty-nine, to keep daily diaries on how often celebrity culture appeared in the media, reality television, and fashion cultures they consumed and how it connected to the world of public and political issues. The researchers then followed up with interviews of the diarists.

Their conclusion was that the world of celebrity and the world of public interest do not talk to each other. When the media's presentation of celebrity stories did lead to discussion from the diarists, it was most likely to be a commentary on how irrelevant they were to genuine public issues—so reaffirming, not redrawing, the public-celebrity boundary.

Those study subjects who closely followed celebrity culture were the *least* engaged in politics and the *least* likely to use their social networks to involve themselves in public issues. Their conclusion: it is important for cultural studies to recognize that popular culture does not always provide the bridge to agreement. The misinformation pervading celebrity culture means that fans can base their beliefs on "truthiness" and "alternative facts" rather than on science-based evidence.

When we wonder why people are bowling alone, and why American politics has become so divided and disarrayed, all we have to do is turn on the television or check our smartphone and watch the celebrities parade by. So it happened that during one week in 2022, when Anthony Fauci was recommending new vaccines and Volodymyr Zelenskyy was pleading for help against invaders, our national conversations were instead dominated by the "slap heard around the world" administered by Will Smith to Chris Rock at the Oscars and the courtroom antics of Johnny Depp and Amber Heard.

The Greeks knew the difference between their immortal gods and their mortal heroes. Whether by cause or by correlation, the media has blurred this distinction and left us a nation of narcissists.

Maria Ressa, the Filipino American journalist who won the Nobel Peace Prize in 2021, has been arrested ten times since starting her iconoclastic digital news website *Rappler* in 2012. The Philippine government shut it down once again in June 2022. "This is illegal," Ressa said. "For me, this is harassment and intimidation. We'll continue doing our jobs. In fact, our end goal is to keep swatting away at that Damocles sword." Ressa argues that the misinformation used by advertisers and internet outlets increasingly promotes authoritarian regimes and suppresses her independent journalism.[10]

The same could be said for the celebrity obsessions that dominate social media and the internet. As Ressa put it in her Nobel Prize lecture, social media "with its god-like power has allowed a virus of lies to infect each of us, pitting us against each other, bringing out our fears, anger, and hate . . . Without facts, you can't have truth. Without truth you can't have trust. Without trust, we have no shared reality, no democracy, and it becomes impossible to deal with our world's existential problems: climate, coronavirus, the battle for truth."[11]

Celebrity is ultimately at the core of an ecosystem that empowers an entire spiderweb of industries, including social media, nightlife, entertainment, fashion, publishing, television, and much more. We are now in the awkward period when we try to look past the newest technologies to see if celebrities can approach the public naturally and honestly, unmediated by intense media coverage. If celebrities themselves can gain the self-awareness needed to do so, there is hope.

There is increasingly evidence this is happening. Consider that in recent years:

> A Swedish teenager with Asperger's syndrome, Greta Thunberg, helped to draw the world's attention to climate change, the biggest issue facing our planet.

A young man from Chicago's South Side, Dewayne Perkins, inspired a generation of gay comedians to change the things people will laugh about.

A twenty-three-year-old transgender model named Valentina Sampaio became the first trans woman to be photographed for the *Sports Illustrated* swimsuit issue.

Ali Stoker, who had a spinal injury and lost the use of her legs at the age of two, became the first wheelchair user to win a Tony in 2019 for her role in *Oklahoma!*

Other stars have deliberately minimized their celebrity status to promote their good works. Some are well-known: Michael J. Fox for Parkinson's; others less so: Roger Federer building schools for girls in Africa and donating money to pay for continued schooling for Ukrainian children, and the singer Ed Sheeran recording a video to raise money for Ukraine. Likewise, dozens of celebrities have signed on to a Global Citizen–organized social media campaign to support the Ukrainian people.

Arianne Phillips, a costume designer for Madonna, asks the key question: "Is it possible to take the fascination with celebrity culture and use it to inspire fans to do good?" Her answer was Red Carpet Advocacy (RAD), founded in 2018 "to change the conversation on the red carpet" so it's not just about frocks and fashion but about frocks and philanthropy. (The fashion brands worn by celebrities on the red carpet will contribute to a designated charity.) Katie Couric and Kim Kardashian captured the polarities of celebrity behavior in a single week in the fall of 2022. Couric publicly and personally discussed breast cancer treatment on the same day that Kardashian paid a $1.26 million settlement to the SEC for illegally accepting payments for endorsing cryptocurrency investments.[12] Both stories were covered extensively and oddly equally in the media.

Perhaps now we can look beyond the economics of scale celebrities bring to media and marketers. Armed with the observable heroics we witnessed in the spring of 2022 in Ukraine, and the example of courageous journalists like Maria Ressa in oppressive regimes, the media can bend us toward what the radio host and author Michael Krasny calls "true honor"— the kind of honor that "does not flow from power, money, or fame. . . . True honor is what we contribute, regardless of being recognized, respected or celebrated. It is what we give to those we care about, friends and family, but also to community and country, those in need and those worthy, both the living and the dead. . . . True honor is and always will be in strength of character and the high-minded and heartfelt deeds that come from it."[13]

That is a gift we can all celebrate.

ACKNOWLEDGMENTS

This voyage of discovery began with the band of thirty-four enterprising journalists who started *People* magazine in 1974, led by their charismatic founding editor, Richard B. Stolley. While working with them, I started taking notes for the book that is now in your hands. That it came to fruition owes first to my perspicacious editor, Helene Atwan, who saw from the start the scope and often worrisome impact of celebrity culture on all of us. I owe more to Helene, Amy Caldwell, and their colleagues at Beacon Press than I can easily express, as I similarly do to my terrific literary agent, Carol Mann.

When I began writing this book I found many guides to help me. The celebrity phenomenon has generated its own literary sub-genre. While much recent interest has come from academic publishers, several general interest books published decades ago remain the pathfinders. Daniel Boorstin's *The Image: A Guide to Pseudo-Events in America* (1961) defined many of the terms still in use today. Richard Schickel's *His Picture in the Papers: A Speculation on Celebrity in America Based on the Life of Douglas Fairbanks, Sr.* (1963) uses Fairbanks as an emblematic case study of Hollywood celebrity. Schickel followed up with *Intimate Strangers: The Culture of Celebrity in America* (1985). Leo

Braudy's *The Frenzy of Renown: Fame and Its History* (1986) tracks the history of celebrity from the time of Julius Caesar and Alexander the Great through the mid-twentieth-century America of Charles Lindbergh and Louis Armstrong. Three excellent studies of mid-twentieth-century popular culture that deal with celebrities are Neil Postman's *Amusing Ourselves to Death: Public Discourse in the Age of Show Business* (1985), Joshua Gamson's *Claims to Fame: Celebrity in Contemporary America* (1994), and Neal Gabler's *Life: The Movie; How Entertainment Conquered Reality* (2000).

The effort to make sense of celebrity picked up steam in the twenty-first century. Kurt Andersen's *Fantasyland: How American Went Haywire; A 500-Year History* (2017) touches briefly on celebrity culture, as does David Friend's *The Naughty Nineties: The Triumph of the American Libido* (2017). Several recent studies focused on individual celebrities are Sharon Marcus's *The Drama of Celebrity* (2019) about Sarah Bernhardt, Antoine Lilti's *The Invention of Celebrity* (2017), about Europe during the Enlightenment and Romantic periods, A. Scott Berg's biography of Charles Lindbergh, and Walter Isaacson's of Albert Einstein.

Robert D. Putnam's *Bowling Alone: The Collapse and Revival of American Community* (2020) was indispensable to me, as was his helpful counsel.

My first researcher, Gunnar Rice, helped me explore the thickets of social media and an array of related topics. So did his colleague, Princeton professor Susan Wolfson, for the Romantic tradition. I relied on Dr. Thomas Singer, a gifted Jungian psychoanalyst, to explicate the ways the ancient Greeks thought about their gods and goddesses and what that tells us about celebrity worship.

Many writer, scholar, and editor friends have discussed and read portions of this book. I am especially indebted to Lorraine Atkin, Gary Alan Fine, Wil Haygood, Henry von Kohorn, Thomas LeBien, Pia de Jong, Robert D. Putnam, Beth Swann, Ed Tenner, Phyllis Ward, and Evan and Oscie Thomas.

Special thanks go to my nonpareil researcher-writers from the Princeton University Department of English: Rebecca Cao, Alan Huo, Ergene Kim, Amanda Kural, Cammie Lee, Andrew Matos, Auhjanae McGee, Grace Rocker, Bethany Villaruz, and Sophia Wang.

None of this could have happened were it not for Drs. Rajiit Rampal and Roni Tamari and their colleagues at Memorial Sloan Kettering Cancer Center in New York. They brought me back from the abyss and gave me the gift of time to tell my wife, Sarah, and our three children—Rebecca, Landon, and Cassie and their families—how much I love them.

NOTES

INTRODUCTION: THE CELEBRITY-INDUSTRIAL COMPLEX

1. Rachel DeSantis, "Richard Stolley, the Man Who Launched People Magazine, Dies at 92," *People*, June 17, 2021, https://people.com/human-interest/richard-stolley-peoples-first-managing-editor-dies-at-92.

2. Daniel J. Boorstin, *The Image: A Guide to Pseudo-Events in America* (1962) (New York: Vintage Books, 1992), 57. Emphasis in original.

3. Taylor Lorenz, "Niche Internet Micro Celebrities Are Taking Over the Internet," *Washington Post*, August 24, 2022, https://www.washingtonpost.com/technology/2022/08/24/nimcel-influencers-tiktok-youtube.

4. Alice Marwick and danah boyd, "To See and Be Seen: Celebrity Practice on Twitter," *Convergence: The International Journal of Research into New Media Technologies* 17, no. 2 (May 2011): 139–58. Emphasis in original.

5. Bradley Bond, "Social and Parasocial Relationships During COVID-19 Social Distancing," *Journal of Social and Personal Relationships* 38, no. 8 (August 2021): 2308–29.

6. *The Poems of Emily Dickinson*, ed. Thomas H. Johnson (Cambridge, MA: Belknap Press of Harvard University Press, 1983).

7. John Naughton, "Daniel Craig: A Very Secret Agent," *GQ Britain*, March 29, 2012, https://www.gq-magazine.co.uk/article/daniel-craig-interview.

CHAPTER 1: HOW IT STARTED

1. Frank Burgess and Landon Y. Jones, "Malcolm X Declares West 'Doomed,'" *Daily Princetonian*, September 27, 1963, https://paw.princeton.edu/article/essay-meeting-malcolm-x.

2. "Malcolm Scores U.S. and Kennedy," *New York Times*, December 2, 1963.

3. Otto Fuerbringer to Hedley Donovan, Andrew Heiskell, and James Shepley, "Revised Prospectus," Time Inc. internal document, August 1, 1973.

4. Scottie Fitzgerald Smith, "Mia Is the Daisy Father Had in Mind," *People*, March 4, 1974, 34.

5. Sheilah Graham, "Seven Parties in a Single Day," *People*, March 4, 1974, 8–9, and "Chatter," *People*, March 18, 1974, 60.

6. Dan P. McAdams, *The Redemptive Self: Stories Americans Live By* (New York: Oxford University Press, 2013).

7. Erik H. Erikson, *Childhood and Society* (New York: Norton, 1950).

8. Tom Vitale, "Gore Vidal, American Writer and Cultural Critic, Dies," *NPR News*, August 1, 2012, https://www.wbur.org/npr/157696354/gore-vidal-american-writer-and-cultural-critic-dies, accessed September 2, 2022.

9. "Laura Sanderson Healy '77: Writing Royalty, a Correspondent's Life," "News Detail," Hutchison School website, January 13, 2022, https://www.hutchisonschool.org/news-detail?pk=1211632.

CHAPTER 2: BREAD AND CIRCUSES

1. Patrick Brantlinger, *Bread & Circuses: Theories of Mass Culture as Social Decay* (London, Cornell University Press, 1983), 22.

2. Rudolf Otto, *The Idea of the Holy: An Inquiry into the Non-Rational Factor in the Idea of the Divine and Its Relation to the Rational* (1923) (London: Pantianos Classics, 2018).

3. Leo Braudy, *The Frenzy of Renown: Fame and Its History* (New York: Vintage, 1986).

4. Nicholas de Chamfort, *Maximes, Pensées, Caractères et Anecdotes*, ed. Jean Dagen (Paris: Garnier-Flammarion, 1968), 66, as cited in Antoine Lilti, *The Invention of Celebrity, 1750–1850*, trans. Lynn Jeffress (Cambridge: Polity Press, 2017), 105.

5. Samuel Johnson, *The Rambler* 165, October 15, 1751, available at https://www.johnsonessays.com/the-rambler/no-165-the-impotence-of-wealth-the-visit-of-scrotinus-to-the-place-of-his-nativity/.

6. Samuel Johnson, *The Rambler*, vol. V, p. 13–17, August 10, 1751, as quoted in Lilti, *The Invention of Celebrity*, 99.

7. David A. Bell, *Men on Horseback: The Power of Charisma in the Age of Revolution* (New York: Farrar, Straus and Giroux, 2020).

8. Bell, *Men on Horseback*, 87.

9. Bell, *Men on Horseback*, attributed to "N. Fisher," the sister of Joshua Fisher, 82.

10. Max Farrand, ed., *The Records of the Federal Convention of 1787*, Vol. III (New Haven, CT: Yale University Press, 1911), https://archive.org/details/recordsfederalc00farrgoog/page/n8/mode/2up.

11. Thomas S. Kidd, *George Whitefield: America's Spiritual Founding Father* (New Haven, CT: Yale University Press, 2014), 260.

12. S. A. Bent, "Lord Byron," *Familiar Short Sayings of Great Men*, 6th ed. (Boston: Ticknor and Co., 1887), available at https://www.bartleby .com/344.

13. "What Is It?" advertisement, *New York Tribune*, March 1, 1860, available at Lost Museum Archive, https://lostmuseum.cuny.edu/archive /what-is-it-advertisement-new-york-tribune, accessed September 2, 2022.

14. Sharon Marcus, *The Drama of Celebrity* (Princeton, NJ: Princeton University Press, 2019).

15. Marcus, *The Drama of Celebrity*.

16. M. A. Root, *The Camera and the Pencil; Or the Heliographic Art, Its Theory and Practice in All Its Various Branches . . .* (Philadelphia: M. A. Root, 1864), quoted in Barbara McCandless, "The Portrait Studio and the Celebrity: Promoting the Art," in *Photography in Nineteenth-Century America*, ed. Martha A. Sandweiss (New York: Harry N. Abrams, 1991), 48–75.

17. McCandless, "The Portrait Studio and the Celebrity," 68.

18. McCandless, "The Portrait Studio and the Celebrity," 72; Joy Kasson, *Buffalo Bill's Wild West: Celebrity, Memory, and Popular History* (New York: Hill and Wang, 2000).

19. "Buffalo Bill for President," William F. "Buffalo Bill" Cody Collection, MS6, MS6.3778.066.05 (1892 London), McCracken Research Library, Buffalo Bill Center of the West, Cody, Wyoming.

20. Kasson, *Buffalo Bill's Wild West*.

21. Kasson, *Buffalo Bill's Wild West*, 123.

22. Jack Halberstam, *Female Masculinity* (1998), 20th anniversary ed. (Durham, NC: Duke University Press, 2018).

23. Karen R. Jones, *Calamity: The Many Lives of Calamity Jane* (New Haven, CT: Yale University Press, 2020).

24. Fintan O'Toole, *Judging Shaw: The Radicalism of GBS* (Dublin: Royal Irish Academy, 2017), 21–22.

25. Jones, *Calamity*.

CHAPTER 3: THE DARK SIDE OF CELEBRITY

1. Frederic Wakeman Jr., *Policing Shanghai, 1927–1937* (Berkeley: University of California Press, 1996), 214.

2. Kai Bird and Martin J. Sherwin, *American Prometheus: The Triumph and Tragedy of J. Robert Oppenheimer* (New York: Vintage Books, 2005), 309.

3. A. Scott Berg, *Lindbergh* (New York: Putnam, 1998).

4. Berg, *Lindbergh*.

5. Berg, *Lindbergh*, 281.

6. Ntozake Shange, *Betsey Brown* (New York: St. Martin's Press, 1985), 34.

7. The full accounts of the Greenlease case are available in the online archive of the *St. Louis Post-Dispatch*, now online at Newspapers.com, and in the FBI interviews in the *Greenlease Kidnapping (Summary Report)* (Washington, DC: Federal Bureau of Investigation, 1981).

8. For excellent histories of the Greenlease crime, see John Heidenry, *Zero at the Bone: The Playboy, the Prostitute, and the Murder of Bobby Greenlease* (New York: St. Martin's Press, 2009), and James Deakin, *A Grave for Bobby: The Greenlease Slaying* (New York: William Morrow, 1990).

9. "The Kidnapping," editorial, *New York Times*, October 9, 1953, 26.

10. Einstein to Max Born, December 8, 1919; Einstein to Ludwig Hopf, February 2, 1920, both cited in Walter Isaacson, *Einstein: His Life and Universe* (New York: Simon & Schuster, 2007), 268.

11. Marshall Missner, "Why Einstein Became Famous in America," *Social Studies of Science* 15, no. 2 (May 1985): 267–91.

12. Isaacson, *Einstein*, 297.

13. Isaacson, *Einstein*, 268: Einstein to Max Born, December 8, 1919; Einstein to Ludwig Hopf, February 2, 1920.

14. Missner, "Why Einstein Became Famous in America," 267–91.

15. Isaacson, *Einstein*, 269.

16. Richard Crockatt, *Einstein and Twentieth-Century Politics: "A Salutary Moral Influence"* (Oxford: Oxford University Press, 2016), 7–32.

17. Crockatt, *Einstein and Twentieth-Century Politics*, 24.

18. Isaacson, *Einstein*, 475, citing Leo Szilard Papers, box 12, folder 5, University of California, San Diego.

CHAPTER 4: WHEN BIG NAMES DID GOOD WORKS

1. Landon Y. Jones, "Liz Triumphant!" *People*, December 10, 1990.

2. Jones, "Liz Triumphant!"

3. For more about this episode, see Landon Y. Jones, "Essay: Former 'People' Editor Recalls Tea with Princess Diana," *Princeton Alumni Weekly Online*, December 11, 2020.

CHAPTER 5: SEX, LIES, AND SOCIAL MEDIA

1. Lebowitz discusses celebrity in *Public Speaking*, a documentary directed by Martin Scorsese that aired November 22, 2010, on HBO, and in Alexandra Silver, "Q&A: Fran Lebowitz on *Public Speaking*," *Time*, November 22, 2010.

2. Ian Halperin, *Kardashian Dynasty: The Controversial Rise of America's Royal Family* (New York: Gallery Books, 2016), 127.

3. Sheila McClear, "That Kim Kardashian and Ray J Sex Tape Was a Huge Money Maker," *Newsweek*, September 13, 2022, and Emma Nolan, "Fact Check: Did Ray J, Kim Kardashian, Kris Jenner Make Sex Tape 'Deal'?" *Newsweek*, May 5, 2022.

4. Cristina Kinon, "E! Renews 'Keeping Up with the Kardashians,'" *Daily News*, November 13, 2007, https://web.archive.org/web/20160304 212354/http://www.nydailynews.com/entertainment/tv-movies/e-renews -keeping-kardashians-article-1.260586.

5. Harriet Ryan and Adam Tschorn, "The Kardashian Phenomenon," *Los Angeles Times*, February 19, 2010, https://www.latimes.com/archives /la-xpm-2010-feb-19-la-et-kardashian19-2010feb19-story.html.

6. "Number of Monthly Active Facebook Users Worldwide as of 2nd Quarter 2022," Statista, August 22, 2022, https://www.statista.com /statistics/264810/number-of-monthly-active-facebook-users-worldwide.

7. Richard Harrington, "Colbie Caillat: A MySpace Star on the Rise," *Washington Post*, August 17, 2007, https://www.washingtonpost.com /wp-dyn/content/article/2007/08/16/AR2007081600730.html.

8. Dave Brooks, "Colbie Caillat Signs with CAA," *Billboard,* July 28, 2021, https://www.billboard.com/pro/colbie-caillat-signs-with-caa, accessed September 11, 2022.

9. Guy Trebay, "Model Struts Path to Stardom Not on Runway, but on YouTube," *New York Times*, February 13, 2012, https://www.nytimes .com/2012/02/14/us/kate-upton-uses-the-web-to-become-a-star-model .html, accessed September 6, 2022.

10. Jan Hoffman, "Justin Bieber Is Living the Dream," *New York Times*, December 31, 2009, https://www.nytimes.com/2010/01/03/fashion/03 bieber.html

11. Carly Olson, "How to Make Money as an Influencer—The Lynette Adkins Way," *Los Angeles Times*, September 23, 2021, https://www.latimes .com/business/story/2021-09-23/content-creators-meet-lynette-adkins -youtube-influencer-marketing.

12. Chris Hayes, "On the Internet, We're Always Famous," *New Yorker*, September 24, 2021, https://www.newyorker.com/news/essay/on-the -internet-were-always-famous.

13. Rachel Nuwer, "Andy Warhol Probably Never Said His Celebrated 'Fifteen Minutes of Fame' Line," *Smithsonian Magazine*, April 8, 2014, https://www.smithsonianmag.com/smart-news/andy-warhol-probably -never-said-his-celebrated-fame-line-180950456.

CHAPTER 6: HOW CELEBRITIES HIJACKED HEROES

1. Landon Y. Jones, "Too Many Celebrities, Not Enough Heroes," opinion, *Washington Post*, February 28, 2014, https://www.washington post.com/opinions/too-many-celebrities-not-enough-heroes/2014/02/28 /dbfc3f5c-98e0-11e3-80ac-63a8ba7f7942_story.html.

2. Evan Thomas, *First: Sandra Day O'Connor* (New York: Random House, 2017), 207.

3. Yalda T. Uhls and Patricia M. Greenfield, "The Rise of Fame: An Historical Content Analysis," *Cyberpsychology: Journal of Psychosocial Research on Cyberspace* 5, no. 1 (2011).

4. CBS News Detroit, "John Lennon's Killer Says He Sought Glory and Deserved the Death Penalty," September 22, 2020, https://www.cbsnews.com/detroit/news/john-lennons-killer-says-he-sought-glory-and-deserved-the-death-penalty, accessed September 11, 2022.

5. Julie Turkewitz and Jess Bidgood, "Who Is Dimitrios Pagourtzis, the Texas Shooting Suspect?" *New York Times*, May 20, 2018, https://www.nytimes.com/2018/05/18/us/dimitrios-pagourtzis-gunman-texas-shooting.html.

6. Drew Pinsky and S. Mark Young, *The Mirror Effect: How Celebrity Narcissism Is Seducing America* (New York: Harper Collins, 2009), 159.

7. From interview with *Dallas Times Herald*, in *What They Said in 1978: The Yearbook of Spoken Opinion*, ed. Alan F. Pater and Jason R. Pater (Beverly Hills, CA: Monitor Book Co., 1979), 336.

8. Luke Chang and Eshin Jolly, "Gossip Drives Vicarious Learning and Facilitates Social Connection," *Current Biology* 31, no. 12 (June 21, 2021): 2539–49.

9. Alice Marwick and danah boyd, "To See and Be Seen: Celebrity Practice on Twitter," *Convergence: The International Journal of Research into New Media Technologies* 17, no. 2 (May 2011): 139–58; DOI: 10.1177/1354856510394539.

10. Marwick and boyd, "To See and Be Seen," 139–58.

11. Thomas S. Singer, a Jungian analyst and scholar, author interview, via email, December 17, 2021.

12. CBS Sunday News, "Mail Call: Donna Reed's Wartime Letters," December 24, 2017, https://www.youtube.com/watch?v=yelcOEG0us4.

13. Henry von Kohorn, "The Hall of Fame for Great Americans," 2021, original draft manuscript. In author's possession.

CHAPTER 7: CELEBRITY WORSHIP

1. Robert D. Putnam, *Bowling Alone: The Collapse and Revival of American Community* (New York: Simon & Schuster, 2020), 206.

2. Andrew Johnson and Andy McSmith, "Children Say Being Famous Is Best Thing in the World," *The Independent*, December 18, 2006.

3. Yalda T. Uhls and Patricia M. Greenfield, "The Value of Fame: Preadolescent Perceptions of Popular Media and Their Relationship to Future Aspirations," *Developmental Psychology* 48, no. 2 (2012): 315–26, https://doi.org/10.1037/a0026369.

4. Jacob Dirnhuber, "Children Turn Backs on Traditional Careers in Favour of Internet Fame, Study Finds," *The Sun*, May 22, 2017.

5. Richard Morin, "What Teens Really Think," *Washington Post*, October 23, 2005, https://www.washingtonpost.com/archive/lifestyle/magazine/2005/10/23/what-teens-really-think/9ffff170-b5e5-4c19-a1d5-c480c9fb00dc, accessed September 12, 2022.

6. R. J. Reinhart and Zacc Ritter, "Americans' Perceptions of Success in the U.S.," *Gallup Blog*, October 2, 2019, https://news.gallup.com /opinion/gallup/266927/americans-perceptions-success.aspx.

7. Robert A. Reeves et al., "Celebrity Worship, Materialism, Compulsive Buying, and the Empty Self," *Psychology & Marketing* 29, no. 9 (2012): 674–79.

8. Jake Halpern, "Appendix: The Rochester Survey," in *Fame Junkies: The Hidden Truths Behind America's Favorite Addiction* (Boston: Mariner Books, 2007), 200–213.

9. Lynn E. McCutcheon and Mara Aruguete, "Is Celebrity Worship Increasing over Time?" *Journal of Studies in the Social Sciences and Humanities* 7, no. 1 (April 2021), 66–75.

10. Halpern, *Fame Junkies*.

11. McCutcheon and Aruguete, "Is Celebrity Worship Increasing over Time?", 66–75.

12. Colleen McClain et al., "The Behaviors and Attitudes of U.S. Adults on Twitter," Pew Research Center, November 15, 2021, https:// www.pewresearch.org/internet/2021/11/15/the-behaviors-and-attitudes -of-u-s-adults-on-twitter.

13. Yalda T. Uhls, "The Value of Fame—Kids and Media," *Psychology in Action*, January 21, 2012, https://www.psychologyinaction.org /psychology-in-action-1/2012/01/21/the-value-of-fame-kids-and-media.

14. Children's Digital Media Center@LA, "I Want My Fame TV: UCLA Study Finds That Tweens Receive a Clear Message from Their Favorite TV Shows: Fame Is the Most Important Value," press release, June 2011, https://www.cdmc.ucla.edu/wp-content/uploads/sites/170/2018 /04/I-Want-My-Fame-TV-CDMCpressreleaseUhlsGreenfieldfinal4.pdf; Yalda T. Uhls and Patricia M. Greenfield, "The Rise of Fame: An Historical Content Analysis," *Cyberpsychology: Journal of Psychosocial Research on Cyberspace* 5, no. 1 (2011).

15. A. Manago, S.-S. A. Guan, and P. Greenfield, "New Media, Social Change, and Human Development from Adolescence Through the Transition to Adulthood," in *The Oxford Handbook of Human Development and Culture: An Interdisciplinary Perspective*, ed. L. A. Jensen (New York: Oxford University Press, 2015), 519–34.

16. Uhls and Greenfield, "The Rise of Fame."

17. Chong Ju Choi and Ron Berger, "Ethics of Global Internet, Community and Fame Addiction," *Journal of Business Ethics* 85, no. 2 (March 2009).

18. Joyce Carol Oates, "Adventures in Abandonment," *New York Times Book Review*, August 28, 1988.

19. Adapted from Andrew Sobel, *It Starts with Clients: Your 100-Day Plan to Build Lifelong Relationships and Revenue* (New York: Wiley, 2020).

CHAPTER 8: THE SELLING OF CELEBRITY

1. Valeriva Safronova, "When Did Every Celebrity Become a Creative Director?" *New York Times*, December 13, 2021, https://www.nytimes.com /2021/12/13/style/celebrity-creative-directors.html, accessed September 13, 2022.

2. Suzanne Kapner and Inti Pacheco, "Gap and Kanye West Are Ending Their Partnership," *Wall Street Journal*, September 15, 2022, https://www.wsj.com/articles/kanye-west-tells-gap-he-is-terminating-partnership-11663246801.

3. Steve Olenski, "Brands, Branding and Celebrities," *Forbes*, April 2, 2018, https://www.forbes.com/sites/steveolenski/2018/04/02/brands-branding-and-celebrities/?sh=317b95d64db9.

4. Kelb Vera, "Dolly Parton Will Give Fans a Chance to Copy Her Iconic Style as She Reveals She's Launching Her Own Fashion Line," *Daily Mail*, May 4, 2019, https://www.dailymail.co.uk/tvshowbiz /article-6992733/Dolly-Parton-fans-chance-copy-iconic-style-announces -fashion-line.html, accessed September 6, 2022.

5. Michael J. de la Merced, "Kim Kardashian's Billion-Dollar Brand Defies the Pandemic," *New York Times*, April 9, 2021, updated June 28, 2021, https://www.nytimes.com/2021/04/09/business/dealbook /kardashian-skims.html.

6. Kurt Badenhausen, "Kobe Bryant's $600 Million Fortune: How He Won On—and Off—the Court," *Forbes*, January 28, 2020, https:// www.forbes.com/sites/kurtbadenhausen/2020/01/28/kobes-600-million -fortune-how-he-scored-onand-offthe-court/?sh=733b683c6d36.

7. Amanda Hess, "What Happens When People and Companies Are Both Just 'Brands,'?" *New York Times*, May 1, 2018; quoting Advertising for Humanity founder Dan Pallotta in the *Harvard Business Review* (2011).

8. Laura Woods, "10 Celebrities Who Have Insured Their Body Parts for Big Money," Yahoo! Finance, March 26, 2021, https://finance.yahoo .com/news/10-celebrities-insured-body-parts-210000413.html.

9. Andrea Towers, "Amanda Gorman Turned Down $17 Million in Endorsement Deals After Inauguration," *Entertainment Weekly*, April 8, 2021, https://ew.com/books/amanda-gorman-turned-down-17-million -in-endorsement-deals.

10. Samira Farivar, Fang Wang, and Ofir Turel, "The Dark Side of Social Media Influencing," *The Conversation*, May 12, 2022, https://the conversation.com/the-dark-side-of-social-media-influencing-181553.

11. Dan P. McAdams, *The Stories We Live By: Personal Myths and the Making of the Self* (New York: Guilford Press, 1993), 35.

12. David S. Heidler and Jeanne T. Heidler, *The Rise of Andrew Jackson: Myth, Manipulation, and the Making of Modern Politics* (New York: Basic Books, 2018), 303.

13. Patrick Radden Keefe, "How Mark Burnett Resurrected Donald Trump as an Icon of American Success," *New Yorker*, January 7, 2019, https://www.newyorker.com/magazine/2019/01/07/how-mark-burnett -resurrected-donald-trump-as-an-icon-of-american-success.

14. Paul Bond, "Leslie Moonves on Donald Trump: 'It May Not Be Good for America, but It's Damn Good for CBS," *Hollywood Reporter*, February 29, 2016, https://www.hollywoodreporter.com/news /general-news/leslie-moonves-donald-trump-may-871464/#!

15. Chris Cillizza, "The Point," CNN.com, April 11, 2022, https:// www.cnn.com/2022/04/09/politics/trump-mehmet-oz-endorsement -pennsylvania/index.html.

CHAPTER 9: THE HUMAN COSTS OF CELEBRITY

1. Melena Ryzik, Nicole Sperling, and Matt Stevens, "A Slap Could Sting the Smith Family Brand," *New York Times*, April 2, 2022 https:// www.nytimes.com/2022/04/02/movies/will-smith-family-oscars-slap .html.

2. Kathryn VanArendank, "The Woman's Redemption Plot," *New York*, February 28, 2022, 64–65.

3. Stephen Sherrill, "Acquired Situational Narcissism," *New York Times Magazine*, December 23, 2001, https://www.nytimes.com/2001 /12/23/magazine/l-acquired-situational-narcissism-727172.html.

4. W. Keith Campbell and Joshua D. Miller, eds., *The Handbook of Narcissism and Narcissistic Personality Disorder: Theoretical Approaches, Empirical Findings, and Treatments* (Hoboken, NJ: John Wiley & Sons, 2011).

5. Christopher Lasch, *The Culture of Narcissism: American Life in an Age of Diminishing Expectations* (New York: Norton, 1979), 10, 21.

6. Although Robin Williams had a history of alcohol and cocaine use, and his cause of death was suicide, an autopsy also revealed that he suffered from Lewy body dementia.

7. Dave Itzkoff, *Robin* (New York: Henry Holt, 2018), 144–45.

8. Jean-Jacques Rousseau, *Rousseau, Judge of Jean-Jacques: Dialogues: The Collected Writings of Rousseau, Volume 1*, ed. Roger D. Masters and Christopher Kelly, trans. Judith R. Bush, Roger D. Masters, and Christopher Kelly (Hanover, NH: University Press of New England, 1990), 128–29.

9. Mark A. Bellis et al., "Elvis to Eminem: Quantifying the Price of Fame Through Early Mortality of European and North American Rock and Pop Stars," *Journal of Epidemiology & Community Health* 61, no. 10 (October 2007): 896–901.

10. Bellis et al., "Elvis to Eminem," 896–901.

11. Jib Fowles, *Starstruck: Celebrity Performers and the American Public* (Washington, DC: Smithsonian Institution Press, 1992).

12. Kenneth Gergen, *Rational Being: Beyond Self and Community* (New York: Oxford University Press, 2011).

13. David Hepworth, *Uncommon People: The Rise and Fall of the Rock Stars* (New York: Henry Holt, 2017).

14. Gina Piccalo, "Celebrities Face the 'Piñata Syndrome,'" *Los Angeles Times*, May 20, 2005, https://www.latimes.com/archives/la-xpm-2005 -may-20-et-breakdown20-story.html.

15. Janet Mock, *Redefining Realness: My Path to Womanhood, Identity, Love & So Much More* (New York: Atria Paperback, 2014).

CHAPTER 10: SWIMMING WITH NARCISSUS

1. Chris Hedges, *Empire of Illusion: The End of Literacy and the Triumph of Spectacle* (New York: Nation Books), 32–33.

2. Joshua D. Miller et al., "Narcissism and United States' Culture: The View from Home and Around the World," *Journal of Personality and Social Psychology* 109, no. 6 (2015): 1068–89, https://psycnet.apa.org /record/2015-43587-001.

3. Statista, "Countries with the Most Twitter Users 2022," July 27, 2022, https://www.statista.com/statistics/242606/number-of-active -twitter-users-in-selected-countries.

4. Mark Young and Drew Pinsky, "Narcissism and Celebrity," *Journal of Research in Personality* 40 (2006): 463–71.

5. Courtland S. Hyatt et al., "Exposure to Celebrities as a Possible Explanatory Mechanism in the Perception of American Narcissism," *Collabra: Psychology* 3, no. 1 (2017): 1–6, 4, DOI: https://doi.org/10.1525 /collabra.52; Lasch, *The Culture of Narcissism*.

6. Hyatt et al., "Exposure to Celebrities as a Possible Explanatory Mechanism in the Perception of American Narcissism."

7. Joseph Epstein, "The Culture of Celebrity," *Weekly Standard*, October 17, 2005.

8. Lynn E. McCutcheon et al., "Conceptualization and Measurement of Celebrity Worship," *British Journal of Psychology* 93, no. 1 (February 2002): 67–87.

9. Zack O'Malley Greenburg, "Michael Jackson's Earnings: $825 Million in 2016," *Forbes*, October 14, 2016, https://www.forbes.com/sites /zackomalleygreenburg/2016/10/14/michael-jacksons-earnings-825 -million-in-2016/#5cfa43c3d720].

10. Sandra Sobieraj Westfall, quoting David Dobson from article by Diane Herbst, "Actor-Turned-President Zelenskyy Is the 'Tom Hanks of Ukraine': 'Fearless' Performer and Family Man," *People,* March 21, 2022, 48.

11. Nataliya Roman, Berrin A. Beasley, and John H. Parmelee, "From Fiction to Reality: Presidential Framing in the Ukrainian Comedy *Servant of the People,*" *European Journal of Communication* 37, no. 1 (2022): 48–62.

12. "Murdoc's Question Answered by Madonna," *Q Magazine*, May 2008, http://allaboutmadonna.com/madonna-library/madonna-interview-q-magazine-may-2008.

CHAPTER 11: STORIES CELEBRITIES TELL

1. Dan P. McAdams, *The Stories We Live By: Personal Myths and the Making of the Self* (New York: Guilford Press, 1993), 35.

2. McAdams, *The Stories We Live By*, 102.

3. Winston Churchill, *The Celebrity* (New York: MacMillan Co., 1898).

4. Warren I. Titus, "Winston Churchill (1871–1947)," *American Literary Realism, 1870–1910*, vol. 1, no. 1 (Fall 1967): 26–31.

5. Michele K. Troy, "Emerging Modernism and the Anxiety of Resemblance" (PhD diss., Loyola University Chicago, 2000), 132.

6. Churchill, *The Celebrity*.

7. Al Morgan, *The Great Man* (New York: Pocket Books, 1956).

8. Sharon Marcus, *The Drama of Celebrity* (Princeton, NJ: Princeton University Press, 2019), 19.

9. Gregg Mangan, "P. T. Barnum: An Entertaining Life," Connecticut History, July 5, 2021, https://connecticuthistory.org/p-t-barnum-an-entertaining-life, accessed May 31, 2022.

10. Brian Horrigan, "'My Own Mind and Pen': Charles Lindbergh, Autobiography, and Memory," *Minnesota History* (Spring 2002), http://collections.mnhs.org/MNHistoryMagazine/articles/58/v58i01p002–015.pdf, 7.

11. Horrigan, "'My Own Mind and Pen,'" 10.

12. Horrigan, "'My Own Mind and Pen,'" 10.

13. Horrigan, "'My Own Mind and Pen,'" 10.

14. Randall Stross, "Edison the Inventor, Edison the Showman," *New York Times*, March 11, 2007, https://www.nytimes.com/2007/03/11/business/yourmoney/11edison.html, accessed May 31, 2022.

15. Stross, "Edison the Inventor, Edison the Showman."

16. Michel Schneider, "Michel Schneider's Top 10 Books About Marilyn Monroe," *The Guardian*, November 16, 2011, https://www.theguardian.com/books/2011/nov/16/michel-schneider-top-10-marilyn-monroe-books, accessed May 31, 2022.

17. Elaine Showalter, "Joyce Carol Oates's *Blonde* Is the Definitive Study of American Celebrity," *New Yorker*, April 13, 2020, https://www.newyorker.com/books/second-read/joyce-carol-oatess-blonde-is-the-definitive-study-of-american-celebrity.

18. Andrew McCarthy, *Brat: An '80s Story* (New York: Grand Central, 2021), 118.

19. McCarthy, *Brat*, 205.

20. Greg Braxton, "'The Bachelor' Made a 'Sideshow' of Its First Black Star. Now He's Speaking Out," *Los Angeles Times*, June 9, 2022, https://

www.latimes.com/entertainment-arts/tv/story/2022-06-09/the-bachelor
-matt-james-rachael-kirkconnell-first-impressions.

21. Katie Couric, *Going There* (New York: Little, Brown, 2021), 176.

22. Couric, *Going There*, 197.

23. Couric, *Going There*, 288.

24. Couric, *Going There*, 294.

25. Couric, *Going There*, 316.

26. Couric, *Going There*, 455.

27. Couric, *Going There*, 483.

28. Will Smith with Mark Manson, *Will* (New York: Penguin, 2021), 1.

29. Smith and Manson, *Will*, 202.

30. Smith and Manson, *Will*, 165.

31. Smith and Manson, *Will*, 164.

32. Smith and Manson, *Will*, 404.

33. Smith and Manson, *Will*, 226.

34. Catherine Shoard, "The Theory of Everything Review: Hawking's Story Packs Powerful Punch," *The Guardian*, September 7, 2014, https://www.theguardian.com/film/2014/sep/07/theory-of-everything-review-hawking-eddie-redmayne, accessed June 6, 2022.

35. Sara Lampert, "Britney Spears's Plight Reflects a Long History of Men Controlling Women Stars," *Washington Post*, February 24, 2021, https://www.washingtonpost.com/outlook/2021/02/24/britney-spearss-plight-reflects-long-history-men-controlling-women-stars, accessed June 9, 2022.

36. Manohla Dargis, " 'Judy' Review: The Singer (Disaster, Legend) at Rainbow's End," *New York Times*, September 25, 2019, https://www.nytimes.com/2019/09/25/movies/judy-review.html.

37. Guy Lodge, "Film Review: Renée Zellweger in 'Judy,' " *Variety*, August 30, 2019, https://variety.com/2019/film/reviews/judy-review-renee-zellweger-1203316871, accessed June 9, 2022.

38. Christy Lemire, "I, Tonya," RogerEbert.com, December 7, 2017, https://www.rogerebert.com/reviews/i-tonya-2017, accessed June 9, 2022.

39. Lemire, "I, Tonya."

40. Manohla Dargis, "Review: 'I, Tonya.' I, Punching Bag. I, Punch Line," *New York Times*, December 6, 2017, https://www.nytimes.com/2017/12/06/movies/i-tonya-review-margot-robbie.html, accessed June 9, 2022.

41. Richard Brody, " 'I, Tonya,' Reviewed: A Condescending Bio-Pic of Tonya Harding," *New Yorker*, December 7, 2017, https://www.newyorker.com/culture/richard-brody/i-tonya-reviewed-a-condescending-biopic-of-tonya-harding.

42. Matt Zoller Seitz, "Jackie," RogerEbert.com, December 2, 2016, https://www.rogerebert.com/reviews/jackie-2016, accessed June 11, 2022.

43. Oline Eaton, "Jacqueline Kennedy Onassis: A Celebrity After-life in American Culture," *Journal of American Studies* 53, no. 2 (2019): 317–32, doi:10.1017/S0021875817001347, accessed June 11, 2022.

44. Michael Carlson, "Ron Galella Obituary," *The Guardian*, June 1, 2022, https://www.theguardian.com/artanddesign/2022/jun/01/ron-galella-obituary.

45. Manohla Dargis, " 'Jackie': Under the Widow's Weeds, a Myth Marketer," *New York Times*, December 1, 2016, https://www.nytimes.com/2016/12/01/movies/jackie-review-natalie-portman.html, accessed June 11, 2022.

46. Dargis, " 'Jackie.' "

47. Guy Lodge, "Film Review: 'Jackie,' " *Variety*, September 7, 2016, https://variety.com/2016/film/reviews/jackie-review-natalie-portman-1201853716, accessed June 11, 2022.

48. Inkoo Kang, " 'Pam & Tommy' Is Good. But It's Hard to Avoid Feeling Queasy," *Washington Post*, February 2, 2022, https://www.washingtonpost.com/tv/2022/02/02/pam-and-tommy-review.

49. Kevin Townsend, Sophie Gilbert, Spencer Kornhaber, and Shirley Li, "Justice for Pamela," *The Atlantic*, February 26, 2022, https://www.theatlantic.com/podcasts/archive/2022/02/pam-tommy/622912.

50. Sydney Bucksbaum, "Pamela Anderson Will 'Never, Never Watch' 'Pam & Tommy,' Source Says," *Entertainment Weekly*, February 11, 2022, https://ew.com/tv/pamela-anderson-will-never-watch-pam-and-tommy.

51. James Poniewozik, " 'Pam & Tommy' Review: The Internet Is for Porn," *New York Times*, February 1, 2022, https://www.nytimes.com/2022/02/01/arts/television/pam-and-tommy-review.html.

52. Poniewozik, " 'Pam & Tommy' Review."

53. Didion quoted in Selma Blair, *Mean Baby: A Memoir of Growing Up* (New York: Alfred A. Knopf, 2022), 11.

CHAPTER 12: SHAPE-SHIFTING

1. Coco Khan, "Cameo Founder on Why Celebrities Offer Video Shoutouts: 'Not All Talent Are Motivated by Cash,' " *The Guardian*, June 30, 2021, https://www.theguardian.com/lifeandstyle/2021/jun/30/cameo-founder-steven-galanis; Mark Caro, "The Most American Startup Ever," *Chicago Magazine*, January 14, 2020, https://www.chicagomag.com/Chicago-Magazine/January-2020/Cameo-Steven-Galanis.

2. Cameo (@cameo), "Introducing a 6th love language for Father's Day . . . ," Instagram video, June 7, 2022, https://www.instagram.com/reel/Cegp-V9JrB9/?igshid=YmMyMTA2M2Y=.

3. Khan, "Cameo Founder on Why Celebrities Offer Video Shoutouts."

4. Alex Hickey, "Cameo CEO Steven Galanis on the New Game of Fame," *Morning Brew*, April 25, 2021, https://www.morningbrew.com/daily/stories/2021/04/25/icebreakers-cameo-ceo-steven-galanis.

5. Khan, "Cameo Founder on Why Celebrities Offer Video Shoutouts."

6. Kara Swisher, "Lifestyles of the 'More Famous Than Rich,'" *Sway*, *New York Times*, December 7, 2020, 3:36, https://www.nytimes.com/2020/12/07/opinion/sway-kara-swisher-steven-galanis.html.

7. Caro, "The Most American Startup Ever."

8. Swisher, "Lifestyles of the 'More Famous Than Rich,'" 3:02.

9. Khan, "Cameo Founder on Why Celebrities Offer Video Shoutouts."

10. Caro, "The Most American Startup Ever."

11. Khan, "Cameo Founder on Why Celebrities Offer Video Shoutouts"; Caro, "The Most American Startup Ever"; Todd Spangler, "Cameo, Celebrity Video Shout-Out App, Lays Off 25% of Its Employees," *Variety*, May 4, 2022, https://variety.com/2022/digital/news/cameo-layoffs-celebrity-video-shout-out-1235258625.

12. Tom Faber, "What Cameo Knows about Celebrity," *Financial Times*, January 21, 2022, https://www.ft.com/content/7d40e262-52e8-4180-9300-472346adec3a.

13. Swisher, "Lifestyles of the 'More Famous Than Rich,'" 11:55.

14. Khan, "Cameo Founder on Why Celebrities Offer Video Shoutouts."

15. Caro, "The Most American Startup Ever."

16. Emily Kirkpatrick, "*The Office*'s Brian Baumgartner Made Over $1 Million on Cameo This Year," *Vanity Fair*, December 10, 2020, https://www.vanityfair.com/style/2020/12/brian-baumgartner-the-office-cameo-one-million.

17. Grace Panetta, "Sarah Palin Earned More from Making Cameo Video Messages Than She Would in Congress," *Business Insider*, May 18, 2022, https://www.businessinsider.in/politics/world/news/sarah-palin-earned-more-from-making-cameo-video-messages-than-she-would-in-congress/articleshow/91649176.cms.

18. Alex Borstein (@alexborstein), "Wow, what an awesome opportunity to get Susie or Lois to say whatever you want!! . . . ," Instagram video, June 13, 2022, https://www.instagram.com/p/CeyJZACgvVT/?igshid=YmMyMTA2M2Y=.

19. Jason Feifer, "Regaining Trust," *Entrepreneur* (July-August 2019), 18.

20. Feifer, "Regaining Trust."

21. "Top 10 Most Popular Podcasts," All Top Everything, https://www.alltopeverything.com/top-10-most-popular-podcasts, accessed August 23, 2022.

22. David Marchese, "Alex Cooper Is Coming for Joe Rogan's Spot," *New York Times*, May 20, 2022, https://www.nytimes.com/interactive /2022/05/23/magazine/alex-cooper-interview.html.

23. Julie Miller, " 'We're Three Complete Idiots': Celebrities Flock to Podcasting for Fun and Profit," *Vanity Fair*, February 4, 2021, https:// www.vanityfair.com/style/2021/02/celebrities-flock-to-podcasting-for -fun-and-profit.

24. Lynette Rice, "Celebrity Podcasts Are Everywhere—and the Deluge of Downloads Has Only Just Begun," *Entertainment Weekly*, January 13, 2022, https://ew.com/podcasts/celebrity-podcasts-boom-seth-rogen -ellen-pompeo.

25. "Entertainers and Celebrities Embrace Podcasting," *Backtracks*, https://backtracks.fm/blog/celebrities-embrace-podcasting, accessed August 23, 2022.

26. "Entertainers and Celebrities Embrace Podcasting."

27. Brad Adgate, "As Podcasts Continue to Grow In Popularity, Ad Dollars Follow," *Forbes*, February 11, 2021, https://www.forbes.com/sites /bradadgate/2021/02/11/podcasting-has-become-a-big-business/?sh= fe70412cfb4b.

28. Adgate, "As Podcasts Continue to Grow In Popularity, Ad Dollars Follow"; "Entertainers and Celebrities Embrace Podcasting."

29. Jeremy Wade Morris, "The Spotification of Podcasting," in *Saving New Sounds: Podcast Preservation and Historiography*, ed. Jeremy Wade Morris and Eric Hoyt (Ann Arbor: University of Michigan Press, 2021), 208.

30. Morris, "The Spotification of Podcasting," 214.

31. Mason Bissada, "Joe Rogan's Spotify Deal Allegedly Worth $200 Million, Doubling Initial Report," *Forbes*, February 17, 2022, https://www.forbes.com/sites/masonbissada/2022/02/17/joe-rogans -spotify-deal-allegedly-worth-200-million-doubling-initial-report /?sh=2f044cea2c39.

32. Jeremy Gordon, "The Rise of the Professional-Athlete Podcast," *New York Times*, July 10, 2022, https://www.nytimes.com/2022/07/06 /magazine/professional-athlete-podcast.html.

CHAPTER 13: "R U REAL?"

1. Special thanks to Grace Rocker of Princeton University for her assistance in helping me understand the topsy-turvy history of Lil Miquela.

2. Elena Block and Rob Lovegrove, "Discordant Storytelling, 'Honest Fakery,' Identity Peddling: How Uncanny CGI Characters Are Jamming Public Relations and Influencer Practices," *Public Relations Inquiry* 10, no. 3 (2021): 272.

3. Aleks Eror, "Meet Lil Miquela, the AI Influencer on the Cover of Our New Print Issue," *HighSnobiety* 16 (April 24, 2018), https://www.highsnobiety.com/p/lil-miquela-cover-story-issue-16.

4. Alexandre Marain, "From Lil Miquela to Shudu Gram: Meet the Virtual Models," trans. Stephanie Green, *Vogue France*, April 9, 2019, https://www.vogue.fr/fashion/fashion-inspiration/story/from-lil-miquela-to-shudu-gram-meet-the-virtual-models/1843.

5. Miquela Spotify page, https://open.spotify.com/artist/7licaqhcEB QUzz9FownRaJ, last updated March 24, 2022; Miquela (@lilmiquela), Instagram account; Yoree Koh and Georgia Wells, "The Making of a Computer-Generated Influencer," *Wall Street Journal*, December 13, 2018, https://www.wsj.com/articles/the-making-of-a-computer-generated-influencer-11544702401.

6. Matt Klein, "The Problematic Fakery of Lil Miquela Explained," *Forbes*, November 17, 2020, https://www.forbes.com/sites/mattklein /2020/11/17/the-problematic-fakery-of-lil-miquela-explained-an -exploration-of-virtual-influencers-and-realness.

7. Koh and Wells, "The Making of a Computer-Generated Influencer."

8. Reid Hoffman, "Episode 66: How to Build Authentic Connection at Scale, w/Trevor McFedries and Lil Miquela," *Masters of Scale*, Spotify, September 2020, 20:55, https://open.spotify.com/episode/6rk9RavVs HN9EDh4wDyvBY?si=8Mxgq_JLRueHdmfIahCpyg.

9. Hoffman, "How to Build Authentic Connection at Scale."

10. Klein, "The Problematic Fakery of Lil Miquela Explained."

11. "Reality Check: TINA.org Calls on FTC to Address Virtual Influencers," *Truth in Advertising Blog*, June 22, 2020, https://truthin advertising.org/articles/reality-check-tina-callson-ftcto-address-virtual -influencers.

12. Samir Chaudry and Colin Rosenblum, "The Curious Case of Lil Miquela," YouTube, 2019, 5:25, https://www.youtube.com/watch?v= i4rwlQ7IA1U.

13. Block and Lovegrove, ""Discordant Storytelling, 'Honest Fakery,' Identity Peddling," 272.

14. Hoffman, "How to Build Authentic Connection at Scale," 36:14.

15. Raymond Blanton and Darlene Carbajal, "Not a Girl, Not Yet a Woman: A Critical Case Study on Social Media, Deception, and Lil Miquela," in *Handbook of Research on Deception, Fake News, and Misinformation Online*, ed. Sergei A. Samoilenko and Innocent E. Chilwua (Hershey, PA: IGI Global, 2019), 94.

16. Klein, "The Problematic Fakery of Lil Miquela Explained."

17. Miquela (@lilmiquela), "We always come with EXTRA SAUCE," Instagram photo, October 17, 2020, https://www.instagram.com/p /CGc6qt3n1M8.

18. Hoffman, "How to Build Authentic Connection at Scale," 4:00.

19. Hoffman, "How to Build Authentic Connection at Scale," 3:41.

20. Miquela (@lilmiquela), Instagram account.

21. Koh and Wells, "The Making of a Computer-Generated Influencer."

22. Bermuda (@bermudaisbae), "OF COURSE Miquela deletes my posts the second I give her the account back. . . ," Instagram photo, April 17, 2018, https://www.instagram.com/p/BhsaN1kHr-x/?igshid=YmMy MTA2M2Y=.

23. Miquela (@lilmiquela), "Hi. I got my account back. I swear this is me. . . ," Instagram photos, April 19, 2018, https://www.instagram.com/p /BhwuJcmlWh8/?igshid=YmMyMTA2M2Y=.

24. "Who Is Bermuda? @bermudaisbae, Explained," Virtual Humans, https://www.virtualhumans.org/human/bermuda, accessed June 9, 2022.

25. Petrarca Emilia, "Everything We Know About Lil Miquela's Instagram Hack," The Cut, April 18, 2018, https://www.thecut.com /2018/04/lil-miquela-hack-instagram.html?regwall-newsletter-signup =true.

26. Miquela (@lilmiquela), "Who can relate?" Instagram photo, May 14, 2018, https://www.instagram.com/p/Bix-NTeB9UV/?igshid= YmMyMTA2M2Y=.

27. Miquela (@lilmiquela), "I've been really stressed since I'm no longer working with my managers at Brud. . . ," Instagram photo, April 25, 2018, https://www.instagram.com/p/BiAVQVHl05m/?igshid=YmMy MTA2M2Y=.

28. Miquela (@lilmiquela), "I'm thinking about everything that has happened and though this is scary for me to do . . .," Instagram photo, April 20, 2018, https://www.instagram.com/p/BhzyxKoFIIT/?igshid= YmMyMTA2M2Y=.

29. Lauren Michele Jackson, "Shudu Gram Is a White Man's Digital Projection of Real-Life Black Womanhood," New Yorker, May 4, 2018, https://www.newyorker.com/culture/culture-desk/shudu-gram-is-a-white -mans-digital-projection-of-real-life-black-womanhood.

30. Rosa Boshier, "This Is Fucky: Simulated Influencers Are Turning Identity into a Form of Currency," Bitch Media, January 28, 2020, https:// www.bitchmedia.org/article/who-is-lil-miquela-racial-implications-of -simulated-influencers-of-color.

31. Boshier, "This Is Fucky."

32. Calvin Klein (@CalvinKlein), "Here at CALVIN KLEIN, we welcome all types of constructive feedback from our community. . . ," Twitter, May 17, 2019, https://twitter.com/CalvinKlein/status/112952104130961 4085; Sandra Song, "Lil Miquela Criticized For 'Sexual Assault' Vlog," PAPER, December 14, 2019, https://www.papermag.com/lil-miquela -sexual-assault-vlog-2641593301.html.

33. Song, "Lil Miquela Criticized for 'Sexual Assault' Vlog."

34. Block and Lovegrove, "Discordant Storytelling, 'Honest Fakery,' Identity Peddling," 277.

35. Blanton and Carbajal, "Not a Girl, Not Yet a Woman," 98.

CHAPTER 14: THE FUTURE OF FAME

1. John Updike, *Self-Consciousness: Memoirs* (New York: Knopf, 1989).

2. Daniel J. Boorstin, *The Image: A Guide to Pseudo-Events in America* (1962) (New York: Vintage Books, 1992), 73–74.

3. "Transcript: John Edwards Interview," *ABC Nightline*, August 8, 2008, https://abcnews.go.com/Politics/story?id=5544981.

4. Thomas S. Singer, author interview, via email, December 17, 2021.

5. Sam Baker, "China Bans Celebrities from 'Showing Off Wealth' or 'Extravagant Pleasure' on Social Media as Communist Rulers Continue Their Crackdown on the Entertainment Industry," *Daily Mail Online*, November 24, 2021, https://www.dailymail.co.uk/news/article-10237617 /China-bans-celebrities-showing-wealth-extravagant-pleasure-social -media.html.

6. John Lie, *K-Pop: Popular Music, Cultural Amnesia, and Economic Innovation in South Korea* (Oakland: University of California Press, 2014), 97.

7. Anoushka Mathew, "BTS Makes History as Their YouTube Channel 'BANGTANTV' Surpasses 70 Million Subscribers," *Pinkvilla*, August 18, 2022, https://www.pinkvilla.com/entertainment/bts-makes-history-their -youtube-channel-bangatantv-surpass-70-million-subscribers-1178298.

8. Joe Coscarelli, "Why Obsessive K-Pop Fans Are Turning Toward Political Activism," *New York Times*, June 22, 2020, https://www.nytimes .com/2020/06/22/arts/music/k-pop-fans-trump-politics.html.

9. Nick Couldry and Tim Markham, "Celebrity Culture and Public Connection: Bridge or Chasm?" *International Journal of Cultural Studies* 10, no. 4 (December 2007): 403–21.

10. Sui-Lee Wee, "Philippines Orders Rappler to Shut Down," *New York Times*, June 29, 2022, https://www.nytimes.com/2022/06/29/world /asia/philippines-rappler-shutdown.html.

11. Maria Ressa, Nobel Peace Prize lecture, Oslo, December 10, 2021, https://www.nobelprize.org/prizes/peace/2021/ressa/lecture.

12. Vanessa Friedman, "Who Are You Wearing and Where Did They Donate?," *New York Times*, January 30, 2019, https://www.nytimes.com /2019/01/30/fashion/red-carpet-advocacy.html; Alex Sundby, "Kim Kardashian to Pay $1.26 Million After Being Accused of 'Unlawfully Touting' Cryptocurrency," *Moneywatch*, CBS News, October 3, 2022, https://www .cbsnews.com/news/kim-kardashian-fined-1-million-by-sec-crypto currency.

13. Michael Krasny, "Kavod, Koved: In Search of Honor," *Moment Magazine*, March 1, 2021, https://momentmag.com/kavod-koved-in -search-of-honor/.

INDEX